# AMAZON FBA

## THE BEST GUIDE TO LEARN YOUR E-COMMERCE FROM ZERO TO SUCCESS.

### PAUL J. ABRAMAH

Amazon Fba

Paul J. Abramah

# TABLE OF CONTENTS

# INTRODUCTION

Sellers have plenty of choices nowadays because a lot of online retail websites have appeared in the market. Individuals can offer their material through numerous platforms and make a fast dollar by offering off their old stuff. You can likewise begin a severe business if that's what you want. The majority of these e-commerce platforms don't care about either method. So making an option in between popular ones can be sturdy.

If you're in for a major company, however, Amazon is the very best option for you. There are many things Amazon makes simple for you. Here are some convincing reasons Amazon is the very best location to begin your e-retail organization:

**Excellent Pricing:**

Amazon provides its sellers a competitive price in the market. Amazon's ASP, or Average Selling Price, for many items is higher than other comparable sites, specifically for the products it sells through FBA (Fulfillment by Amazon). Another terrific thing at Amazon is that clients that appear on there are searching for options and ease of shopping, not for the least high priced or very unique products.

**Simplicity:**

The interface Amazon supplies to its sellers is understood for its sophistication and simplicity, similar to its client platform. When linked

1

to other e-retail platforms, it's more efficient and professionally proficient. With Amazon, things are a lot easier for you since you don't need to work with several third-celebration platforms like PayPal, you can even eliminate the majority of your responsibilities, like listing the item, managing your fees, getting issues delivered, and shooting high-quality images for your details. Amazon makes everything in the skill work correctly for you.

**Presence:**

It's much more difficult for little sellers to get an appearance on their own and their items on most e-retail platforms. They start as a small part of this substantial system, and it's tough to succeed. Amazon provides little sellers with a much better presence than any other platform. This is since Amazon uses a rotating search algorithm, which keeps shuffling search results for consumers from time to time, offering brand-new sellers better exposure. If you can manage to, you can even purchase sponsored links, which will drive a lot more traffic towards your products and improve your sales. You'll make good sales if you have a reliable product.

**No Fee:**

Most people who have operated in this company before having a reasonable concept about the margins. They're tight, aren't they? That's the main factor why every seller desires to decrease his listing costs. As soon as again, Amazon comes to your aid and saves you cash. On Amazon, you don't need to pay any listing cost at all for most items. Some particular types still need a listing cost, but it's so minimal compared to other platforms that you'll happily pay it. Since your upfront costs are lessened, this assists you to keep your stock flexible.

**Easy Order Fulfillment:**

Most e-retail platforms do not care about your shipping requirements and how you're going to have the ability to ship your items to the consumers on time. Amazon is unique, and it makes your headache it's own! Amazon will take care of all your orders by fulfilling them for you if you so desire. You do not have to work hard to fulfill orders yourself or preserve links with satisfaction partners. Amazon carries the responsibility for you, making your job more natural and the system running more efficiently.

**Overhead Costs:**

Overhead expenses are unavoidable in any organization, and every seller desires to decrease them. Amazon emerges as a champ for the sellers here, too. This makes Amazon one of the most affordable platforms available today.

# CHAPTER 1

# Mindset

We live in a material world, and having one job may not cover all of your expenses and leave you with a small discretionary fund, let alone money for emergencies.

If you want to increase your income and you've been thinking about online selling, then perhaps it's time to stop thinking about it and take action.

One thing that is common to many people is that they don't like to take risks. They are very cautious and like to settle for less if they know that the income they will get will cover their expenses and satisfy their needs. However, expenses and needs may vary over time and, unfortunately, the value of your income may not keep up with your needs. Perhaps you are very happy living on your own; you have an average salary and you have a decent life. But everything may change if you meet that special someone and decide to build a family together. Suddenly, priorities change, and there are other needs and expenses to cover. Do you think that your salaries combined will cover these expenses? What if a baby comes? Financially speaking, you will need a lot of money for the years to come as your family grows.

You will have to be pretty inventive in finding an additional income source, or you need to find a way to get a substantial salary raise to cover your needs. Even if you have a six-figure annual salary, or perhaps you are lucky enough to earn even more, why settle for this? This is a major difference between the mentality of an entrepreneur and that of an employee. A true entrepreneur will always think that there is no such thing as enough and doesn't want to settle for less when they can do a lot better.

Settling is something that you have to do in your personal life, but this doesn't apply to your professional life. In a career, you are always looking to climb the corporate ladder. An entrepreneur will always look to earn more money, so settling sounds like retiring.

As mentioned in the introduction, trade is the most profitable business activity there is. Becoming successful on the Amazon platform is a continual learning experience, as you need to know all of the ropes. The competition is fierce, and you will need to discover the best strategies and techniques for advertising, SEO, and sales to stand out from the rest and to be one step ahead of your competitors.

This is written with the intention of providing you with everything you'll need to know to start an Amazon storefront and to remain competitive.

# CHAPTER 2

# Advantages of Amazon FBA

Using Fulfillment by Amazon offers huge benefits for sellers like you. Here are the best benefits you can get by using Amazon FBA:

### 1- Accessibility to the Prime Members

As an online seller, you couldn't ask for a better customer. These Prime Members subscribe at least $99 a year in order to take full advantage of the free shipping that Amazon has to offer.

These Prime Members are not only loyal customers, but they are the ones who tend to purchase items that are more expensive and buy at least %150 more than any of the non-Prime Members. To see these in number basis, they spend around $1,340 on Amazon annually, while non-Prime Members spend only around %529

The use of FBA allows for a wider customer base. There is a speculation of around 50 million Prime Member subscribers in Amazon right now. If you think about, that's a lot of money.

### 2 - The Care for Shipping, Returns, and Customer Service

Amazon handles everything from picking the item, packing it and shipping it to your customers. Quick and swift shipping gives you happy customers and with happy customers provides with increased sales.

Amazon will also be able to handle any of the unsatisfied customers. This will definitely save the time and money for you because you won't need to employ any additional customer service reps.

Since your items will be stored in Amazon's fulfillment centers, you won't need to gain the headache of where to get the space to fit your inventory.

### 3 - Buy Box Win

Those in FBA, depending on the category of the product, can place its price at least 10 – 20% higher than the average competitor and still be able to win the Buy Box. That is if you are using FBA and your competitors are not.

This is because shipping is added into the cost. If your items are priced at $20 with a Prime Member shipping, it will beat out a merchant item of $15 with $5 shipping.

### 4 - Increased Volume of Sales

This may not be a guarantee, but it has been found that those who switch over recognize a rise in unit sales volume to about 20% more. Numerous amounts of sellers have reported higher or even double of their original volume. This is mainly due to the Prime Member subscribers.

## 5 - Customers are Inclined to Pay More for the Same Product

The millions of Prime Member subscribers on Amazon will know a great deal when they see it. As mentioned in one of the benefits, sellers who are in FBA could factor in the cost of shipping into the price. Some Prime Members are willing to pay a few more bucks to be able to ensure that the delivery is prompted in two days and the added convenience.

## 6 - No Such Thing as an Inventory Limit

Since Amazon does your inventory for you, you can sell as much as you want without the worry of the amount of storage requirements that you need.

# CHAPTER 3

# Starting Your Business With Fba

Fulfillment by Amazon (FBA) is often considered a subset of the dropshipping industry with a few major differences. Whereas with traditional dropshipping a third party is responsible for the sourcing and fulfilment of the orders, merchants in a Fulfilment by Amazon relationship send their items to Amazon who is then responsible for storing and shipping the items in question in return for a portion of the profits from the sale of the item.

In addition to making the physical transaction part of an online sale much less of a hassle, those who participate in the FBA program also get preferential treatment when it comes to search results as well as how their packages are shipped. Amazon power users who take advantage of the Amazon Prime membership option receive free 2-day shipping on countless products that Amazon sells directly, but also, on all of the items sold by those in the FBA program.

This means that by simply signing up for FBA you are already placing your future products at a huge advantage when compared to similar products that you will one day be competing against. The amount you are charging for shipping will also affect your Amazon rating in several ways, but suffice it to say, a lower shipping cost is always better. This, coupled with 2-day shipping, goes a long way towards creating positive mindshare, even if your product costs a little more, or is of a new private label brand that the customer has not yet heard of.

How It Works

It is important to understand just how valuable the fact that Amazon is fulfilling the orders in question is, especially when it comes to private label products from a new company. The Amazon name carries quite a bit of weight with customers, and having that name involved in the transaction will make them much more likely to go ahead and pull the trigger on the transaction in question. While they will hopefully become a loyal follower of your brand someday, being an FBA member gets you in the door. Studies show that FBA sellers typically see as much as a 30 percent boost in sales compared to more traditional sellers.

In return for the perks, FBA members pay a $40 monthly fee as well as a percentage of the sale price of each item. You will also be required to pay fees related to the weight of the item when it comes to shipping, any handling fees, pack or pick fees and storage fees based on the square footage. Additionally, you will be required to pay fees related to individually labeling all of your products as you will not want them commingled with other similar products as this will only dilute your brand. If you are unsure if this fee structure will fit the private label products, you may be hoping to one day sell you can check out the revenue calculator available on the official FBA site to determine if your idea is likely going to be a success.

When it comes to fleshing out your business plan it is important to factor in the benefits in terms of exposure that you will likely receive as well as any costs you might incur. This is especially true if you are going to be creating your own product line as you are going to need all of the potential customers you can get. If your initial idea does not appear as though it is going to work with FBA, you may want to consider alternative types of products as the solution is out there, you just have to do the work and find it.

A private label brand is any brand that it is not owned by a major company or organization. Over the past 20 years, private label brands have seen nearly double the growth of more mainstream brands, and the growth in niche markets where the importance of individual ingredient lists is much higher; much like customer interest levels when it comes to getting to know the creators of unique brands.

This is in large part due to the greater amount of perceived control that goes along with these types of products and it is something you can use to your advantage if marketed properly. What's more, when you decide to create your own private label you will have complete control over the branding and marketing of the product in question, allowing you to create something truly special that speaks directly to your target audience. Additionally, you will have the added advantage of perceived value as you don't have to deal with all of the added waste that comes from working with a major brand.

# CHAPTER 4

# How To Create And Register Your Own Brand And Label

A mazon gives you a huge opportunity to earn money online by selling there. You can make some additional income from it, or you can even stop your job and established a full-time service on Amazon if you desire to. This gives you a quantum of freedom can secure more than what you put into it.

**Let me note down a few of the why you should be selling on Amazon:**

- Versatile work schedule and freedom of work
- Financial security
- Excellent returns on your financial investments
- More downtime to enjoy the things you like doing
- Experience to perform bigger jobs in future

You have control over how successful your business will be. Slowly, you will likewise find out the ins and outs of the trade, and this will improve your income further. Making an Amazon Seller Central account is your first action to starting your company.

The process is quite simple. Amazon has provided useful ideas to get you through it quickly, and you do not need to follow anything else. I'll streamline the procedure for you here:

Open the following URL in your web internet browser" sellercentral.amazon.com.

There will be a login tab; click on the login page. "Register Now" button on the login board, it will direct you to a various page.

The first thing to do here is to choose whether you will be selling as an "Individual" or as a "Professional. Let's look at the distinctions between these two.

An Individual seller can sell an optimum of 40 products per month. An Expert seller, on the other hand, can sell any variety of products in a month. There are no constraints.

An Individual supplier is charged a commission of 99 cents on each product that he sells. There's no monthly fee in this case. Rather than that, a Professional seller pays a regular monthly cost of $39.99In in both cases, and you may have to pay for some extra charges at times, like referral costs & variable closing charges.

Professional sellers can sell items in all classifications offered on Amazon. Individual sellers can't do that. They're enabled to offer in just restricted variety of classifications. It's recommended that you go with the "Professional" strategy for your business.

When you choose a strategy, you will need to check out a seller contract and sign it.

Print out this contract before you go any further. This will help you straighten out any problems in the future. As soon as you've read it, consent to the conditions, and after that continue even more.

In the next phase, you will be required to fill out some important details, like your charge card details, billing address, seller name, and your business address.

After this, you will need to confirm your identity. A PIN will be offered to you through a text or a phone-call on a number that you offer them. This is a guideline which lots of sites follow.

A Professional seller likewise needs to supply the required tax info to Amazon in order to continue.

As soon as you've offered your tax info, the registration treatment will be total and you'll be taken to the web page of your Seller Central account. From here, you can handle all activities in your account.

There are several tabs in the leading navigation bar of your home page. Let me provide you a walk-through of these tabs.

**Stock**: You can include new items and manage existing ones from here.

**Reports:** This tab lets you see all your payment reports and tax details.

**Orders**: Check all the received orders and manage all the returns from here.

**Efficiency:** All the feedback you get from clients is shown here along with any claims made by them and other performance-related details. **Settings**: In this webpage, you can change any account information.

## Establishing Your Seller Profile

When your account has actually been activated, you will require to finish your public profile. This is what potential clients will take a look at so consider it as the Amazon version of your Facebook or Twitter profile. Your clients will learn more about who you are, what your organization is all about and what you give in terms of shipping. They will see your revenues policy; they can see feedback from other customers and a lot more besides.

**The primary parts of your profile that you ought to concentrate on are:**

### - About Seller

You need to tell individuals who you are, how your business to begun, what was the motivation behind it. Talk about your business viewpoint, what you want to use and achieve to your consumers and tell them anything else that is appropriate.

### - Your Theme/Logo

Potential customers will be able to see your logo design in some locations, including the Offer Listing page, on your shop and on your At a Glance page. Keep your logo design to 120 x 30 pixels and do not include any URLs or recommendations to your site in it.

## - Your Return and Refunds Policies

Provide your consumers full guidelines on how they can return products for a replacement or a refund. Let them know the address they need to send go back to and inform them around for how long it will take you to send out or process a refund out a replacement item. When you are setting up your goals bear in mind that Amazon has a requirement that all potential sellers customers to return products for a minimum period of 30 days after the sale.

With this info in hand, you can produce your Amazon Seller Central account, start listing your items and earning money!

Amazon desires you to start a business and profit on its site. If you earnings, Amazon profits. As long as you follow the guidelines, Amazon stays on your side. Amazon will if you need help

The site is packed with FAQs and assist files, and assistance is simply a mouse click away. Through its click-to-call feature, you need just click the Call Me button under the Phone tab in the Contact box, appearing on numerous seller-related pages. An Amazonian will call you best away. You'll get instant live assistance to resolve the trouble and get you back to work.

It may look like with all the millions of online sellers; all the great concepts have been taken-- that there's absolutely nothing brand-new under the sun. Well, we've been following "the online market" given that 1984, and e-commerce particularly since 1997, and you take can take our word for it-- chances are plentiful. If you couple a good concept with clever sourcing and excellent client service, you'll be well on your method to success.

# CHAPTER 5

# How To Find The Best Selling Products

This is the most important step in the entire procedure. It will all be for nothing if you stop working on choosing a killer item. Why is it so important? Simply because the only way for your service to prosper is for you to select a theme that offers well. For a product to sell more, it needs to be marketable. Without a terrific product, you can't make your business work. So what makes an item "excellent"? Let's take a look at some essential elements.

**Good Sales Volume**

This is a primary guideline for choosing a great product. You want to give this item, so you require to be sure it is selling well in the market. If you select a niche item that only sells many units each month, you will not be benefiting from it at all. There is too much rivalry in the marketplace, so you must choose an item that is selling huge. It's also essential that you make sure there are no big gamers in the market currently selling that product. These sellers tend to dominate the marketplaces they're offering in, using up many of the market shares by costing low margins. This is because they delight in the economies of large scale that little sellers can't.

## Attractive Pricing

If you're acquainted with a behavior principle called spontaneous purchasing, you must know how essential it is to put the best price on your product. For that, you require to choose a product that falls under the best price bracket. It must be priced high enough that people do not believe in it as an ineffective ornament but need to be inexpensive enough that individuals feel the desire to purchase it as quickly as they see the rate. This is what we call impulsive buying. When the client believes the price isn't high, she doesn't think about making contrasts with similar products, which provides you a competitive benefit.

Considering that you need to pay some costs to Amazon, you can't pick a very cheap item, since you will not benefit from it. The very best cost variety is between $20 and $100. If you want to improve it even further, select an item listed below $50.

## Specific niche Product

Exceptionally generic items will not sell, a minimum of not for your business. So if you were thinking about going with clothes or soap bars, drop the idea. Your products require to be a bit unique so that they can serve a specific niche. Markets of generic items are highly saturated already, and they have huge players dominating the field, so you don't wish to go there. Instead, what you require to do is target a particular group of customers, a group that isn't too huge or too little, but just the right size to offer you rewarding returns. Offer a product that people do not easily find in grocery stores or shopping centers in every city, something that isn't mainstream.

## Non-Seasonal Product

Don't choose a seasonal product, comfortable. If you wish to offer throughout the year, pick an item that is not seasonal. If you can't do away with an annual product, select a few other things to offer, too, and make sure some of them are non-seasonal.

## Needed Competition

A small seller like you can not manage to spend much on advertising your product, so it's great to have some competition in your market. Being the only performer in the market won't help you because you will not be able to produce awareness for your product in the market.

So choose a product that has a healthy level of competition. This will make sure that you can profit far above your competitors' marketing. At the very same time, watch out for oversaturated markets. Too many competitors will eliminate your company, as gone over earlier.

## Good Supplier

Great providers are vital to a company like this. On the other hand, a lousy provider will be undependable, which can hurt your business if he doesn't provide on time.

It's ideal to have an apparent seller for your item( s), and most elegant to have multiple suppliers. That method, you can ensure your sales aren't obstructed even if one seller is dealing with some concern.

## Shipping

The mobility of your item is likewise an essential element. You ought to pick an item that is easy to ship since Amazon enforces strict standards when it comes to packaging and shipping.

## Success

This is the most apparent one. What's the point of offering a product if you can't benefit from it, right? In the end, you're in business to make a profit, and without a valuable item, you can't do this. So make specific the product you select to sell enables you decent revenue margins, even after paying the Amazon costs.

Now that we've looked into some crucial consideration determining what item to offer, you all must be questioning how to find the best product. Let's provide you a head start.

The most convenient way to begin is by looking at the Amazon bestsellers page. Ultimately, you will discover an item you can easily brand name and start selling.

There's the Movers & Shakers area, and a Hot New Releases area on the site, both of which inform you about items that are selling well at the minute. Make a little list of questions, and then put each one through the criteria we studied above. This will assist you in preferencing the best item to offer.

There are other locations to try to find possible items if you're still not satisfied.

Examine eBay, Google Shopping, and other popular eCommerce websites.

Here's a little checklist of things you ought to do when choosing a product:

- Check the demand of the item by going through the bestsellers list or using the Google
- Keyword Tool.
- Make sure the item isn't seasonal.
- Check that the product is properly priced to encourage spontaneous buying.
- Inspect that there are no vast gamers in the market currently selling that item.
- Make sure you can quickly deliver the product.
- Make sure that there are excellent suppliers on the ground for the product.
- Feasibility Checklist

Now, some Amazon sellers seem to be able to get; however, judge the market nothing else ideal and still make money. Together with whatever else in this chapter, I am giving you another method to make sure that you get the best product and the right market, a way of scoring your options to see if you ought to go ahead or call it quits before you lay out any money or time.

The following list is simple to utilize and will help you to figure out if your item is viable and if your market is viable. The system will inform you whether you ought to continue with your private label endeavor or keep on searching. Each line has a rating next to it-- either provide yourself that score if you can answer yes or zero if the feedback is no. In the end, we will total the points and see how far you've gone.

**Viability of the market**

**Is the name of the national brand dominant in the market?**

If your product is in competitors with a nationwide brand name, then, in all honesty, you may too quit. Let's state you select to opt for electronic cameras; the likes of Nikon and Canon would hurry you into insignificance. Think of choosing items such as kitchen area accessories or any other kind of accessory where there is no national trademark name controlling the market

**Is the Average Sales Price Between $15 and $60? Rating 5:**

One crucial point to remember is that you require some margin to spend on your marketing. If you sell something worth $50, you will need to do the same quantity of work as you would if you were selling items that disappeared from $7 to $10. Unless you are running a well-known department store, you will find it hard to win Low profit / high volume action.

**Are Sales rated for the top three products below 10,000? Rating No. 4**

When you choose an item to sell, you need to make sure that there is adequate volume to meet the objectives you set for earnings. Products in the variety of 8000 and 10,000 are offering between 4 and 6 products per day; those in the 5000 to 8000 range will sell between 6 and 10, those that rank in between 200 and 5000, around 10 to 20 products daily and Those who run below 2000 are selling more per day than you can count.

## Do the Top 3 Products have 400 or Fewer? Score 4

Reviews are exceptionally essential in getting a ranking for your item and in convincing prospective consumers that they need to purchase from you and not from a rival While it's possible to get more than enough. Four hundred evaluations, it will take you a good deal of time, effort and, maybe most notably, cash.

If numerous products have less than 400 reviews, you have an essential possibility to act and overtake them, utilizing your excellent marketing abilities.

## Exist Any Page One Products with 100 or Fewer Reviews? Score 5

There is cash to be made from products that fall outside of the leading three positions on page one. It might be that position number 6 or 7 can still earn you a prospective $1000 or more dollars per month, and there aren't a lot of people who would turn their noses up at that, every single month.

You have the best chance of getting on page one when there is an affordable number of items that have 100 or fewer reviews.

## Are There Multiple Keywords for the Market? Score 5

Is your market likely to browse for your item using a variety of various keywords? The more keywords you have, the easier the opportunity you have at making more sales. For instance, if you were offering cutting boards, some people would browse using the words "chopping boards." By utilizing excellent marketing skills, you can end up ranking for several different keywords and raise your sales and your profile considerably.

## Are all Pay Per Click Advertisements in Use? Score 1

Have a look at your rivals- are they on the side or the bottom page PPC ad for long durations? If they are, it implies that they are making good cash from them, and that is another market opportunity to sightsee.

## Is There any Product Video on Page One of the Google Search Results for the Top Keyword? Score 3

If there isn't, then obtain hectic on making a video. Produce yourself a YouTube channel, if you have not currently got on and made some videos of your product. You could discover yourself being ranked on the Google search engine result and adding links to your videos will send people straight to your product page on Amazon.

You can utilize a tool like Merchant Word to find this out. Do use it because this is an excellent way of ensuring that there are enough searches to make your item feasible.

## Can You Increase the Value of Your Product? Score 4

Make use of the issues they raise to make your product a better one. Can you attach some accessory to your line, perhaps bundle two items together or use good discounts for purchasing more?

## Are the Products That Are in the marketplace Durable? Score 5

If the products are breakable or not developed to last long, like things made from glass, they tend to break when they are being distributed. Instead of blaming the shipping company, the client will always lay the blame at your feet and provide you bad assessments. It isn't your fault, but while this keep occurring, your sales will never increase.

## Is the Product Easy to Use Without Complex Instruction Manual? Score 3

If a purchaser does not comprehend how to use your product, it will always be your fault. Go back to the cutting board we were talking about.earlier-- a necessary item that requires no user and no instruction manual.

## Does the Product Lead to More Reorders or orders? Score 5

Can you resell your item to the same customers over and over? Will they keep on returning for more? That is the easiest method to increase your business monthly.

## Can the Product be Offered as a Gift? Score 3

The most significant market nowadays is present getting. If you can get your packaging to appear like it is for a current product, and the product itself is giftable, sales will rise rather considerably. You could find people purchasing for themselves and then reordering as gifts for other individuals.

## Is the Product Something that Can not Easily Be Purchased somewhere else? Score 2

Commodity products, like that regular cutting board, can be bought anywhere, especially in big chain shops, and they are things that many people will purchase from their local markets. If you were to turn that cutting board to something unique, with features that customers can't get somewhere else, they would pertain to buying.

## Product Viability.

## Do the products weigh a pound or less?? Score 4

The smaller sized a product is, the lighter it will be, generally. The brighter an item is, the less it costs to deliver from your provider, and the lower your Amazon charges will be.

## Is the Product Small? Score 4

Picture a product that is about 8 inches by 8 inches by 8 inches; holding your hands together will typically provide you a concept of how huge this is. Now believe about your item; is it more significant than that or smaller size? If it is shorter than that, you can probably obtain into the lowest cost bracket on Amazon, which suggests more cash in your pocket.

## Can the Items be More Outstanding with Well Packaging? Score 5

Product packaging is a massive part of this company. Great packaging motivates more sales and a higher cost. Make your product packaging appealing and appropriate for the product.

## Can You Buy Your Good with Shipping for 20% or Less of the Resale Price? Score 4

Amazon charges include their commission is 15% of your sales cost, handling fees, and packing cost starts at $2.50. If your item has a sales rate of $15, you will lose $2.25 in commission and about $2.50 for Amazon fees, leaving you $10.25 per product.

## Can you Make the Foremost Purchase of 500 Units or Less? Score 4

You do not desire to be laying out every cent you have on your initial order, but do you require adequate products in stock to cover promos and sales until you get sufficient money together to buy more. Purchasing excessive will eliminate your earnings stone dead.

# CHAPTER 6

# How To Create And Optimize The Best Landing Page

## Branding Your Products on Amazon

Since you have placed the order for your products, it's now time to prepare them for sale. You probably are thinking of things related to packing, labeling, and sending your products over to the Amazon's fulfillment centers. But product preparation involves a lot more than that, so you also need to consider branding. This is a fundamental aspect, as you will need to make sure that nothing can stop you to sell these products on Amazon so you have the rights to sell them. When you are a third-party reseller, selling products on this platform can get more complicated than you anticipated.

**This is why you will need to consider the following scenarios:**

Lately, there have been quite a few cases of unauthorized sellers that caught the attention of Amazon. By unauthorized sellers, I mean merchants who continue to sell on this platform although they don't have the rights to do so. It may happen that you don't have full control over your inventory, meaning your products can fall into the wrong hands, so there might be some merchants selling your products without your approval. Obviously, you are not seeing a dime of these sales, so this is where things can get problematic. Unfortunately, not everyone selling on this platform complies with Amazon policies.

It's really hard to imagine something worse for a brand than the situation when there is price transparency, but the authorized sellers don't have command over the price. You might be selling your product at a determined price, and suddenly comes another merchant who sells your own product at a lower price, even though you didn't allow him to do so. Customers are very influenced by the price, so if the product is identical, he will buy cheaper, and not from you.

Fortunately for you, there is a way to avoid this nightmare. You can find a way to protect your brand on Amazon and avoid your products being sold without your consent. This is why you should register a trademark. However, in some cases this may not be enough, so you will need to get some legal counseling to come up with a "bulletproof" trademark. There are still scenarios where the unauthorized sellers can get away with selling your products, but this is where your legal counseling should make the difference. A common practice for the unauthorized sellers is to invoke the "first sale doctrine," which apparently is a legal concept that can allow anyone in a country to buy a product and resell it to whoever (and whenever) they want. This doesn't sound fair, does it?

There are so many different ways to define and implement a trademark capable of protecting you from any unauthorized sellers, especially when they invoke the first sale doctrine. Therefore, to tighten your trademark, you will need to follow the guidelines mentioned below:

1. Tighten your grip over the distribution process so you don't have to send cease-and-desist letters to any unauthorized resellers.
2. Demonstrate that the continued sale of your products without your approval is a legal issue.

It's hard to think of any brand that has absolute control over their distribution process, so their products might fall into the hands of these kinds of merchants. However, by following the tips mentioned above you can aim to minimize this issue, so you will benefit from the sales of your products.

## SEO Strategies to Improve Your Rankings on Amazon

If you are familiar already with the Amazon platform, then you probably know that it functions as a search engine, so from this point of view, you can compare it to Google. However, Amazon's search algorithm is a bit different compared to the one of Google. People come on this platform to search for products and read reviews as well, and Amazon knows this fact. This platform is the main source of information for people searching for products. They come on this website, search for products, read reviews, compare prices, and on plenty of occasions they buy the products they were looking for.

When you are selling on this platform, your main objective is to boost your conversion rate. People might see your products, but it's up to your content if they decide to buy or not. So, yes, your products need to become more visible on this platform. Since Amazon is working like a search engine, when a user types in something in the search query, the website will display results according to rankings, reviews and so on. This is why it's important to get your product to fall within the first few pages of search results. This is where SEO strategies come into play. SEO means Search Engine Optimization. Therefore, everything related to your content has to be optimized to become more visible on the Amazon platform. There are three main objectives you need to aim for when applying SEO strategies:

- visibility - so that your potential buyers can easily see your products in the results.

- relevance - your products will need to come up when searching with keywords. Therefore, your content will show that your product is relevant to the search query.

- Conversions - getting users to view your products is one thing, convincing them to buy your product is another thing. Everything related to your content will need to turn a view into a sale.

There can be three different approaches when it comes to optimizing your products:

- the product approach
- the performance approach
- the anecdotal approach

## The Product Approach

If you simply want to optimize your product listing, then you definitely need to try this approach. But what exactly you need to do in this case? Your product listing is composed of the following elements:

- the title

- the meta-description

- body

- images

The title will need to contain information about brand, type, size, color, quantity, or packaging. Keep in mind that the search query may contain keywords that can be found in your title. Your title will have to contain keywords, but they have to appear in a natural way, so choosing the order of the elements mentioned above is crucial. The title doesn't have to be an enumeration of keywords without having any meaning or sense; it has to be a natural flow of words that will attract potential buyers.

The number of characters in a title may be different, depending on where the product is placed. Let's just suppose that your product is placed in the organic search section (the section which mostly relies on keywords and 'pure' optimization to influence the rankings). In this case, your title can have between 115 and 144 characters. Sounds very long, right? But every word can matter in this case, so make sure you use them wisely. However, things are a bit different in the sponsored section (advertised products), where the title can only have around 30-33 characters, for the mobile version of the platform, or 55-63 characters for the full desktop version of the website (Wallace et al, 2019).

The meta-description will also have to include keywords, and it has to be composed in a very appealing way. This description will be seen by your potential buyer even before clicking on the link to get to your page. It has to be something that will catch the attention of any user.

You'll want to have a call-to-action. This is a sentence or two that will entice the consumer who is browsing to click on your product to learn more. The call-to-action is equally as crucial as your keywords. Some sellers have paid dearly to have a professional write their call-to-action blurb, and it has paid off dearly for them. You might pay $50-100 for a well-written call-to-action or you might pay $2o0, but whatever the cost, a professional will write something that will definitely drive traffic to your store front. And that's what you want, especially when first starting out.

If you peruse Amazon, you will notice that some sellers have a call-to-action, also known as CTA, and others don't. Check the sales of both in your niche and compare sales. You might be surprised to see those with a CTA have many more sales. A catchy sentence or two, or even three, can make all the difference in sales, and it will help you to rank higher in search.

When it comes to the body, this is where you have to be very specific, as the user is expecting product specifications, benefits or other valuable information. Make sure that the information is very well-structured (bullet points will score you some points), extremely well-written, and packed with keywords. If you have a passion for storytelling, you can use this to your advantage, as everybody likes a good story so why not include it in this section?

The images that you are using have to be very professional (a white background can help), as they need to present very clear images of your product (at least 500 x 500 resolution).

But let's get to what really matters. Keywords, keywords, keywords! Technology can be very useful to find the most popular keywords or some very specific keywords. I'm not going to name some of these tools (there are plenty of good tools out there), but you will need to use these apps or plugins to:

1) Research two or three of the most trending keywords applicable to your product.
2) Find out what keywords your competitors are using. There are even tools for such tasks.
3) Go after the competitors with the most reviews. Find out their secret, what keywords they are using, and go through their reviews to understand why the product is so popular.
4) Collect three to four sets of data, mix them together and rule out the search terms not applicable to your products. Then you will know exactly what keywords you have to use in your title or meta-description, but the body as well.

Additionally, you can also use some plugins, extensions, or tools to compile the best title for your product that includes relevant keywords, but also it's very appealing and pleasant to read.

## The Performance Approach

If the product approach is all about focusing on optimizing the content of your product listing, and it mostly relies on Organic SEO, the performance approach is doing your best to boost your product rankings. Your rankings are determined by your sales and reviews. The tricky part is that you need reviews to generate sales, and you need sales to generate more reviews. So these two terms are very dependent one on the other. Perhaps all of the third-party sellers present on this platform have their content optimized, but the result page is not infinite, it can display 10, 25 or a few more results. Can you guarantee that your products will be on the first two pages when the results are being displayed? If you are using just Organic SEO, then you will have serious doubts about this.

In this case you might risk your product to end up on page 18, where nobody even bothers to check it. Now you are probably wondering how to steer traffic to your page? Well, Amazon can give you a hand, but it will cost you. Basically, the performance approach combines the 'pure' SEO strategies with advertising or other alternatives to steer traffic to your product page.

You can get reviews during the pre-launch phase of your product by sending it out to a few people and asking for their honest opinion. Assuming they all collaborate, you can end up with your first reviews, possibly most of them positive. When applying this method, you will have to be careful not to violate any rules or regulations of the Amazon platform. But as long as your product doesn't officially launch with 100 reviews, then you will not have problems with Amazon. Therefore, you can use the pre-launch to get your first reviews and to boost your rankings.

Again, it is stressed that you don't want to have any bogus reviews posted to your account. Keep it honest.

Since this platform is mainly focused on customer satisfaction, proving to them that you are committed to this goal can only help you with your rankings. Not all sales will lead to reviews, so in some cases you may have to be a bit perseverant to follow-up with the customer and ask for an honest feedback. You might get it or not, but at least you are trying. Your efforts will definitely lead to more reviews, and this will help you with your rankings.

Nothing influences more a potential customer than feedback. Reviews (feedback) are considered social statements about the product experience, its quality, features, specs, delivery or even customer service provided. A potential buyer will check your product specifications, the product photos, and if they like what is shown, they might consider buying the product.

## The Anecdotal Approach

This approach is all about using all the tips and tricks on how to properly optimize your content on this platform. So, you will need to take a look below to find them:

1) Consider using FBA
2) Use brand names in your product listings
3) Include the seller name as well
4) Don't forget to fill in other fields in the edit product page
5) Use high quality photos to boost your conversion rate and rankings

## Advertising on Amazon

We have to admit that using just pure SEO techniques will not help you too much nowadays as most likely every merchant on this platform (at least the serious ones) are working hard to optimize their content. But where SEO has its limits, advertising can come along and help you to boost your product visibility and rankings. Using paid advertising will get you the views you need, but you need to make these views worth it to seriously increase your conversion rate. Optimized content will help, but the most decisive aspect that turns a view into a sale is the feedback.

Advertising has the job of promoting your product, but it's not forcing users to buy the product. But to understand the duality of advertising, you might want to check the lines below:

- The PPC (Pay-per-Click) element is the first phase of the sale, since it makes merchants bid on keywords to secure a very good spot on the page. PPC Advertising makes a lot of money for Amazon, so you can understand why this company is allowing third-party resellers to trade on this platform. It's absolutely normal for Amazon to make a large portion of its money from this PPC Advertising process.

- The second phase is when the displayed product gets sold, so the view turns into a sale (a process called conversion). Guess what! Amazon charges a fee for many sales on this platform, and again the company wins a lot of money.

In fact, Amazon manages to score a triple win, if you really think about it, as it:

- Helps the user to find the best match for the product that he or she is seeking, so the platform gets more users, and more people willing to spend their money.

- Boosts the rankings of the seller based on the searched items (PPC Advertising, plenty of money here).

- Takes a fee for sales (if they are done from Individual Accounts).

Increased competition has convinced many sellers to use paid advertising, otherwise, they couldn't be one step in front of the rest. In the past, organic SEO was simply enough to have a better ranking and eventually more sales. But different needs require different solutions, so there has to be a way to differentiate the merchants on this platform as most of them are already optimizing heavily their content. Some of them have become extremely skilled at running paid advertising campaigns just by following the principles below:

- Finding the best keywords to bid on

- Bidding wisely

- Using higher and higher budgets for advertising

- Using experts for this kind of service

An advertising campaign will not guarantee you incredibly high sales, as we are not talking about an exact science. There are plenty of factors that can influence your sales, and advertising plays a key role in this whole process. This is why you will need to find ways to maximize the efficiency of each advertising campaign.

# CHAPTER 7

# Best Strategies For Launching Or Rewiewing Your Products

## Launching Products With Amazon

With everything in place and your products arriving at Amazon's warehouse, it is time for you to launch your products! Launching products on Amazon is actually incredibly simple, but it does take some practice to memorize each of the steps and have a big impact on each launch. As well, you will find that each launch grows as you go because you are better at it each time, and you already have some credibility established around your brand and your reputation. The momentum between your own knowledge and this recognition will help each launch do better than the last, so long as you grow with the momentum.

In this chapter, we are going to go through a simple launch sequence so that you know exactly what you need to be doing in order to succeed with your brand. As you launch your first products, follow this sequence exactly so that you are able to get everything done. Make a note of anything you feel you could do differently to accentuate your strengths and do better, though, so that you can create your own launch sequence that perfectly fits your business and keeps you growing.

## Optimizing Your Listings

The first thing you need to do to launch your product on Amazon is to optimize your listing. Since Amazon works like a search engine, just like Google search does, using SEO is important. This will help your listings show up toward the top of the page, meaning you are more likely to get viewed over the people who fall later than you in the listing rankings.

The best way to SEO your product page is to use relevant search terms in your title and your product description, without going overboard or being spammy about it. Amazon actually has a clause built into their algorithm that prevents people from ranking well if they put too many keywords in their listing. Amazon assumes that these listings are spam and then ranks them incredibly low, preventing them from ever getting found by anyone who is using Amazon to shop. The key is to use keywords sparingly, and in a way that actually makes sense in the flow of your listing.

A great way to spot rich keywords that you could use for your listing is to use a keyword search tool such as Keyword.io or Google's built-in keyword app. Both of these will give you the opportunity to search for keywords that are relevant to your industry so that you can use the best keywords on your listing. Each keyword tool will have its own way of ranking the quality of keywords, so make sure that you follow this ranking to find keywords that are going to be supportive in helping you get found. Typically, these ranking tools will help you avoid keywords that are saturated or ones that are not used enough to really be worth the effort of fitting them into your description.

It is also important that you do not overuse a single keyword in your description. Using a keyword any more than 1-2% of your total description can result in you being marked as spam and your posts not being shown. Find ways to use relevant keywords without overusing them by choosing alternative words, too, so that you can stay optimized in the search parameters.

## Outlining Your Launch Strategy

Once your product listings are all set up and optimized, and your store is ready to go, you can outline your launch strategy. It is crucial that you do not start a launch plan until after your entire shop is set up and ready to go, as doing so could result in you not having everything ready come your chosen launch date. Pushing back launches to accommodate tech glitches or malfunctions is incredibly unprofessional and can massively destroy the momentum of your launch, so avoid that by preparing everything first.

With everything prepared, you can go ahead and create a schedule that will outline your strategy. Ideally, your schedule should include the date that you want your shop ready by, the date that you will start organic advertising, the dates that you will start paid advertising (and what types of paid advertising will be started when) and the dates that you will monitor your growth for important metrics in how you can improve momentum. Having all of this outlined in your schedule in advance will ensure that you know exactly what needs to be done on every day leading up to the official launch of your product so that you can stay on track and continue building momentum.

As you will quickly learn, momentum is the backbone of any strong launch, so having a strong flow of momentum building up around your products and business is essential. You want to build up momentum around your launch, as well as use that building momentum from each product to carry into your next product launch so that you can get ahead each time.

Note that when you launch your first products, you are also going to be launching your store for the first time. For that reason, you should use all of these strategies for the items that you think are going to be most popular, and for your branded store in general. This way, you are promoting both your store and brand itself and the products that you are going to have for sale. This will build momentum and recognition around both your brand and your products, making for a much more successful launch right from the jump. In future launches, you will not have to do as much work around promoting your brand to really get your name out there.

## Launching Your Advertisements

As I mentioned previously, Amazon has three different types of advertisements: sponsored product ads, sponsored brand ads, and sponsored display ads. You are going to want to make use of sponsored product ads and sponsored brand ads at the very least, but ideally, you should use all three to really get your name out there and make the biggest impact in your launch.

Below, I will discuss how all three of these ads work and what you need to do to configure them for your launch.

**Sponsored Product Ads**

Sponsored product ads are the advertisements that are featured at the top of search listings when a customer searches for a product that they want. This type of ad is excellent to launch after you have officially launched your product on your store, as it will help your product appear over anyone else's in search rankings.

You can make a sponsored product ad on Amazon by choosing which product you want to sponsor and following the step-by-step process of designing your ad. Ideally, you should sponsor the products that you think will be most popular so that your money is spent well on these advertisements.

When it comes to creating sponsored product ads, you will go to the product you want to sponsor and tap "sponsor product." Then, you are going to set your target in terms of who your purchasing audience is so that Amazon shows your ad to the right people. You can find out who your target audience is easily by looking at your industry as a whole to get a feel for who is a part of it, and by looking at existing products in other people's store to get a feel for who their audience is. Set your parameters around your findings.

Once your target is organized, you can choose your budget, or how much you want to spend on your ad. Naturally, the more you spend, the more you are going to get seen. However, avoid spending more than you can reasonably budget for so that you are not wasting your money. Ideally, your sponsored product ads should account for 30-50% of your entire ad budget for all of the ads combined. So, if you sponsor three products, each product will receive 1/3 of that total portion of your spending budget.

## Sponsored Brand Ads

Sponsored brand ads appear the same way as sponsored product ads, and they work the same way, too. The only difference with a sponsored brand ad is that you are sponsoring your brand and not a specific product, so you are going to have only one single sponsored advertisement to reflect your entire brand.

Your sponsored brand ad will likely have a similar target audience as your product posts have, as your products and your brand itself will have the same audience. You can use the information you found from your sponsored product ads to determine the parameters of your sponsored brand ads.

When it comes to setting your budget for your sponsored brand ad, your brand ad should take 30-50% of your total advertising budget as well. This way, plenty of people are going to be exposed to your brand so that should they not find your product ads, they will find you.

## Sponsored Display Ads

Sponsored display ads are the advertisements that appear on other people's websites, such as on blogs. Using sponsored display ads is a great way for you to reach other people's audiences so that you are more likely to drive traffic to your own page. You can create a sponsored display ad if you want to increase your reach with your

Amazon store. However, the minimum budget for this option is generally $15,000, so it may be beyond most people's reach.

Creating a sponsored display ad is not done on your own, so if you want to use this feature, you will need to contact an Amazon ad consultant to be shown the process. A qualified consultant will help you determine if your budget is going to reasonably manage a display ad, and it will help you discover what the steps are for you to get your post sponsored in the first place.

## Promoting Your Products

Promoting your products through paid advertisements is not the only way to get your name out there. Promoting your products on your own through word of mouth, known as organic advertising, is another powerful way for you to get your brand out there so that people can interact with your shop and purchase your products.

You should start organic advertising and product promotions at least two weeks before your products launch, as this gives you enough time to talk about your products and build your momentum. Generally, you can start your organic promotions as soon as your shipping procedures are finalized and paid for so that you can feel confident that everything will be in place for the launch date that you are giving your audience. You can promote your products organically on any social media platform through posting and talking about your products on a consistent basis.

The best way to really promote your products and brand this way is to take pictures of your sample products and talk about them and demonstrate them for your audience. As you do, focus on building engagement by asking questions and encouraging people to follow your page so that they can stay up to date on your launch. This way, they are able to get early access to your products the minute they land.

## Reviewing Your Process

After you have launched your products, it is always a good idea to stop and review your launch process. Look over how each step of the process went and jot down any notes you have about how you could have made it go better or what you can do it make it smoother in the future. The more you can keep track and adapt this process to fulfill your own needs and understandings, the easier it is going to be for you to have a smooth launch process that works every single time. This way, launching becomes easier and easier, and your products sell out faster and faster. As a result, you will be earning a far higher income in the end.

# CHAPTER 8

# How To Maximize To Use Amazon Advertising

Whether you work as a marketer or you have been living under a rock, it is almost impossible to miss the ads that pop up on the computer, on billboards, or in any written material. Applications have been made to block ads on your phone or computer because they have become so prevalent in today's society. Why? Because they work.

Customers not only expect to see ads on online shopping sites, but they often respond well to the stimulus. That is because people who enter shopping sites like to see other products for sale. Amazon ads are no exception to the rule. Since it is one of the leading shopping sites in the world, creating ads on Amazon is an excellent way to introduce new customers to your product. And since you are already an Amazon FBA member, you can take advantage of the easy-access advertisements Amazon provides.

**What Are Amazon Ads?**

Amazon ads are paid, sponsored items that pop up as a result of keyword searches. When you search for an item on Amazon, the platform generates a paid advertisement that coincides with your search. For example, if you wanted to find a purple food that induced long episodes of laughter, you might find advertisements that correspond to "purple," "drink," or "laughter." In this case, the results yielded products related to food coloring and humorous mugs.

Ads are designed to optimize the results of Amazon searches, so be aware of the keywords you use when describing your product. Amazon will use those keywords to make the best possible matches with customer searches.

## Are Amazon Ads Worth It?

Consider the last time you spent time on Amazon. Were you swayed by some of the advertisements listed on the home page, or did you make it to the advertisements listed on individual search pages? Either way, it is likely that you have clicked on an ad sometime in your experience with Amazon. So, is it worth it to advertise on Amazon when you have an FBA account? Absolutely! You are already set up with a platform that is designed to help you sell your products, so utilize all the tools that Amazon offers.

Ads generate more clicks for your products, and general studies have noted that interest in your products rises considerably when advertising with paid ads (Whitney, 2019). If you are a first-time seller and do not know where to start with paid advertisements, consult your market research to find trending products. Often, products with these advertisements will also give you a leg up in discovering your own methods for paid advertisements.

## Amazon Advert Costs

Like most online advertisements these days, you can set a budget for your ad. That means that you can choose how much you want to spend and how much time your ad will run. So, if you decide to pay $5 over the course of one day, Amazon will provide you statistics that will let you know how many people you will reach on average. You can adjust your budget or day limit to make use of the estimated number of clicks.

On average, a click costs no more than $0.35. That means that your advertisement will bring a potential customer to your shop for every $0.35 you spend. That is a fairly good average, and it is a great way to get exposure.

## Self-Serve Ads vs. Premium Ads

If you perform a Google search, you will likely see two different kinds of ads; one is listed among the options in the Google results, and the other is listed in the banner on the side or bottom of the page. Self-serve ads are those that are listed with the results. So, if you find yourself looking for a product with keywords similar to those searched, the advertisements would be listed on that page.

On the other hand, premium ads are usually those that have photographs and are glaringly obvious during a search or in search results. For example, if you search for hyena products, you will undoubtedly find many people with interesting views of hyenas, but you might also see an advertisement for Blow Pops listed on the side, tempting you.

## Types of Amazon Ads

Though we have discussed the styles of ads you might see when creating an ad with Amazon, there are three main types that you can select when advertising with Amazon. Each accepts payments with different methods, and each should be used according to different marketing strategies.

## Amazon Sponsored Product Ads

These are the most common types of ads not only on Amazon, but also on the internet. Customers navigate to your page by finding products within a search. As discussed previously, these ads respond to keywords, phrases, and lines. They correspond with links to specific products.

If you are new to Amazon selling, you may want to start with this option. Remember, you sell products, not themes. Once you sell your product efficiently, you can move on to more products. Sponsor your product by searching for common keywords used in competitor sites. Once you have decided on the keywords that best describe your product and get the most traffic, set up your sponsored product ad accordingly.

When paying for a sponsored product ad, you must set a daily budget. Again, you may choose the money you wish to put into an ad, but be smart when considering how many people the ad will reach. For example, if you set a high budget for a single day, you may find that the day you selected is not the best to sell your merchandise. Setting up an ad to sell paint on a Tuesday may be less effective than doing it on Thursday, since more people are interested in home projects on the weekends. Allow the two-day shipping time for the product to reach your customer and decide which time is best to sell your product.

## Headline Search Ads

Headline search ads are often associated with links to other sites or company pages. For example, you may see a headline search ad for a whisk-making company located at the top of a page with search results for kitchen supplies. These ads are often available for a date in the future, so you have time to organize your advertisement and subsequent product before it is released. Headline search ads are also keyword based, so you will not see an ad for a cucumber slicer on the same page as a security system unless you have an abstract way of protecting your home.

This ad is a pay-per-click, which means that every click on the ad costs the company money. These ads are known as campaigns and have a minimum budget of $0.10 per keyword. You must pay at least $100 to display these ads, and the minimum cost per day is $1.00.

When it comes to marketing, you would often use these types of ads to inspire others to visit your shop. This suggests that you have a brand already set up with a variety of options. Unlike the sponsored product ads, you may advertise for your whole inventory, so use this ad when you have built up a good backing. Since the prices for running one of these ads are generally higher, be prepared to shell out a decent amount of money to run it.

## Amazon Product Display Ads

The final type of Amazon ad is the product display ad. Unlike the other two, customers are led to various products through other product detail pages. If you visit Amazon and select a product, you will notice that the ads listed on the page often offer products that are similar to the products or include similar interests. For example, a runner looking for ankle weights might find an ad for running shoes. Amazon uses interests and keywords selected from a long list of options to provide the perfect example for all customers.

Using this ad is a good marketing technique for both new and seasoned sellers. The best way to utilize this type of ad is to do market research on the most common interests and uses for products related to yours. However, since there is a potential list from which to choose, your market research need not be as intense. Instead, take some time reviewing products that are similar to yours.

## How to Optimize Amazon Ads

Like the product listings, it is necessary to optimize Amazon ads to get the most out of your money. Optimizing ads is slightly different than providing keywords for your products, but they do have remarkable similarities. For both, you want to utilize the tools on Amazon to find the best companies to emulate, but instead of placing all keywords in your ad, you must bid on the best keywords. Some keywords are used frequently, so they often cost more than less-used versions. Always be aware of the best ways to show your products. Below are six ways to optimize your Amazon ads and make selling that much easier.

## Organize Campaigns

It may seem like a no-brainer that you must organize how you will submit your campaigns, but there is often more to it than meets the eye. For example, not only do you have to find the best times to produce your ads, but you also must find the best words to use in your campaign. This is commonly called an AdWords account structure. You define the words that would most benefit your campaign and use them in advertising.

Let us look at an example. If you own a business that specializes in cell phone sales, you may have three main categories: Apple, Samsung, and Motorola. These three categories can be broken down even further to specialize in each brand. The Apple Brand may break down into iPhone X, iPhone 8, and iPhone 7. Samsung might have subcategories that include the Galaxy Note10, Galaxy S10, and the Galaxy A20. Motorola may be divided into subcategories such as Moto G, Moto Z, and Moto One. All of these phones have their own subcategories, which may include storage, RAM, etc.

The breakdown of each of these categories provides its own unique set of keywords that can be utilized in ads. Create several ads that support each keyword to get the most exposure.

You will see an increase in sales if you research how much each keyword is used in popular sites. Visit well-known company sites and do a keyword search. Though many company pages will have some of the same keywords, sift through these to find keywords that will match your ad.

## Create Compelling and Urgent Ad Copy

No one wants to read about a product that simply explains why the seller thinks the product is so great. Though it is a good idea to include details in your copy, remember that people from all walks of life will be reading it. You want to be able to reach as many people as possible in as short a time as possible. People are more likely to click on a product if they do not have to slog through all the literature.

Though you want to reach as wide an audience as possible, marketing in too wide a market will often result in fewer clicks as your copy does not answer questions about the product. Keywords come back as a seller's best friend because the more specific you can become with your copy, the more likely people are to see what you have to say.

Create an urgent desire for your product. If you are selling shoe inserts, find out the problems most people have with their shoes and capitalize on them. Advertising a shoe insert as a solution to bad posture may not seem like the best option, but advertising that the insert will help to solve back problems will encourage customers to visit your product's page. People looking for solutions to problems are more likely to write down the symptom than the remedy when searching for products.

## Create Specific Ads

We cannot stress enough that being specific in your product descriptions and ads is one of the best ways to create an ad that will stick in customer's minds. Most people do not search the web by typing "yellow" into a Google search window. Buyers are looking for specific solutions to their problems.

Keywords such as "phone" or "paint" may put you on a search list, but you will likely only have the spot on the 1,000th page. Instead, consider narrowing the search area by adding adjectives and adverbs. For example, key phrases like "16GB phone" or "primer paint" narrow down the search considerably.

## Bid on Popular Brands

It may seem overwhelming to compete with big-name brands such as Maybelline or North Face, but you can use these brands to get ahead in the advertising game. For example, instead of using words like "furniture," select a large brand like "IKEA." Since these brands are often at the top of lists, it is more likely that your brand name will appear with the big dogs.

If you have a rather specific niche and are looking for the top competitors for more unique items, simply type a general term into a search engine. The results will yield ads from other companies (good signs that they have enough cash flow to afford ads on Google searches) and you will likely find articles that rank the best brand names in the biz.

## Experiment with Ad Formats

Though we have specified which marketing technique works with each of the brands, do not be afraid to experiment. In fact, spend your marketing time doing just that. Though it may seem as though product sponsored ads are the only way to go when marketing for the first time, try a different option and compare the results. You may find that you like one version over the other.

The different ad formats reach shoppers in different ways. For example, though some like to find the ads at the top of their list of results, others may find it more helpful to find another product by clicking on an ad within the product details. Use your experience and survey others to see what they look for in an ad.

## Use Negative Keywords

Negative keywords prevent buyers from viewing your ad because it does not match the keyword. For example, if you were to sell hummingbird homes and someone searched for home interior, they may see your ad, which would be a waste of a click. Your ads are only shown to so many people, depending on your budget and time frame. To prevent this from happening, use negative keywords to prevent accidental clicks. You may choose the word "kitchen" or "bedroom" to exclude any searches that may contain those keywords.

Often, when you use negative keywords, you are inadvertently also preventing your products from showing up in large, generic searches, which may also save you a view. The ads you optimize through this method often are marketed for specific results, so choose your negative keywords wisely.

## Conclusion

Amazon ads are some of the best utilized in the business, and since you are now a fully-fledged Amazon seller, take advantage of some of the best technology out there. Consider what you can do when you stake a place for yourself in one of the world's leading online shopping companies.

If you are concerned about whether you should advertise with Amazon ads, the answer is still a resounding yes! Not only could you get more bang for your buck by launching ads specific to your products, but you will also gain much-needed exposure. Remember that your products are only as valuable as you make them, so give them the star treatment.

There are three types of Amazon ads: sponsored product ads, headline search ads, and Amazon product display ads. Each is unique in its opportunity to reach several types of audiences. If you feel as though you are going to break the bank with this venture, do not worry. You can often choose the amount of money you want to spend on each ad and select the right time frame for you.

Optimizing ads, just like optimizing your products, is one of the most beneficial ways to encourage new customers to see your products. Make sure your ads are organized or you will never know which ads perform well for which products. Organize your ads into keyword research, and apply two or more ads to every subcategory to find out which type of ad works best. Remember, do not be afraid to experiment.

Be specific in your ads, and bring in the use of other brand names to make your brand pop. Even though you may not sell North Face jackets, you can always market your products as items similar to them. These specific keywords associated with big brands also narrow down the amount of general information customers have to sift through in order to find your product. The use of negative keywords also helps to prevent general terms from using your clicks.

# CHAPTER 9

# Scaling your Amazon FBA Business

In this part, we will discuss how to make an email list for your blog. On the off chance that you converse with any effective blogger, they will reveal to you the significance of having an email list. Having somebody's email will enable you to get in touch with them decisively. It is more probable for individuals to see and tap on your email than it is for them to get some answers concerning your most recent post online which implies you can't neglect the intensity of email and email promoting.

I will show you today how to gather messages through free traffic and pop-ups. Gathering email can be a tedious and an arduous procedure, yet vital.

I will do my best to make it basic for you. Keep in mind that building a decent email rundown will require some serious energy. Additionally, on the grounds that you have figured out how to gather 10,000 messages doesn't mean every one of them will tap on your email.

You have to ensure you are keeping your messages endorsers connected with and hanging tight for the following email, which we will show you in this section. Ultimately, we will additionally manage you on the most proficient method to make probably the most astonishing messages. It will assist you with getting a higher snap through rate. Despite the fact that email showcasing is great, just 30% of individuals will peruse and click your email. We need to ensure we leave no stones unturned to do that and we need an elegantly composed email.

## Collecting email

Toward the start of your blogging venture, you won't have a lot of cash to spend on promoting. In this section we will keep everything free assets, which means, you won't need to pay a dime on gathering any messages. Presently there are two fundamental ways for you to acquire messages. The first is through a spring up.

You can utilize email assets like MailChimp to make a free spring up. What spring up will assist you with is the point at which somebody visits your site, they will get a major box directly before them. It will approach them to agree to accept our email list so they could get a free book or something along that line, as we discussed in the past section. Contingent upon your specialty give your readers something of significant worth.

In case you're in the wellness Niche, you can offer your readers free eBooks on the most proficient method to put on muscle. Make sense of the considerable number of requirements and issues individuals have in your specialty. Make a free eBook or a cheat sheet and offer them for nothing. It is an absolute necessity have on your site. Odds are if individuals are on your site as of now, they won't falter to put their email in pop-ups with the expectation of complimentary data.

## Your Landing Page

Presently the second method to gather messages is use something many refer to as a greeting page. When you join with mailchimp.com. which is allowed to utilize, you would then be able to begin making free points of arrival for your site. What presentation page will do is help you gather messages through YouTube and different destinations. In the past section, we discussed gathering messages through YouTube. This is the place points of arrival come in.

Make your presentation page through mailchimp.com. At that point duplicate that connection and post it on your YouTube recordings and different sites on the web. Your presentation page will offer a blessing in return for their email. So in the event that you go on to wellness structures and specialty sites you can gradually include your point of arrival there to explicit individuals who are into your specialty. It is additionally an amazing route for you to gather messages on your YouTube recordings and other specialty related sites. You need your point of arrival there ready for action. On the off chance that not, at that point you are passing up a ton of free leads.

## Making email

At long last, the fun part, how to make an email and how regularly you ought to send messages to your readers. So the main thing you have to ensure is that you have your appreciated email computerized. In case you're utilizing the administrations, we prescribe mailchimp.com. You ought to have no issue robotizing email since it is exceptionally direct.

At whatever point somebody agrees to accept your email list, the main thing you have to do is ensure you are sending them the blessing you have guaranteed. Your "appreciated" email will be the main robotized email, ensure your "appreciated" email is sent following they enter their email. This would be your robotized email, since you have made you're free to email and computerized it, we will currently discuss the recurrence and the sorts of email you ought to send your supporters.

As to rate, you ought to never email your readers multiple times each week. There are two explanations behind it. To begin with, you will have a lower possibility of winding up in their spam email. Second, your readers won't get irritated by your messages. Subsequently, they won't withdraw.

With respect to messages, update them about the most recent blog and the partner items you need to offer them two times per week. This is a decent principle guideline I like to live by. Not exclusively will they be locked in on the information you give them, yet they will probably turn into your clients. It won't resemble you're shelled with deals pitch constantly. Subsequent to attempting this for quite a long time and years, I can reveal to you this is the best technique for messaging your readers.

On the off chance that you need to have an effective blog, you need your readers drew in through email. You can lose online networking following, yet the messages will live on until the end of time. Some should seriously think about email medieval, however most organizations are running exclusively on email showcasing. Try not to belittle the intensity of email promoting, particularly for bloggers.

Utilize these techniques we just discussed in this section to gather messages. Try not to leave any stones unturned on the off chance that you need to make progress in blogging.

## Guest Blogging

Presently there are several things to recall before you begin posting your online journals on other individuals' sites. The main thing you need to ensure is that you have a few online journals all alone website before you post on others. Let's be honest, nobody needs new bloggers to post on their site, get a few certifications and compose an incredible blog or two develop a resume. When you've figured out how to post two or three online journals all alone website, at that point you can begin reviewing visitor writes so as to create more traffic and to get some reputation in your specialty.

The sooner you begin visitor blogging, the better it will be for your image. It will enable you to make more backlinks, however it will likewise enable you to draw in more readers to your blog. Another extraordinary thing about this strategy is that if the site you posted on gets new readers, the odds of the new readers to visit and turn into a reader of your blog would be exceptionally high. Presently you should simply discover individuals who will enable you to post on their site, that is the thing that we will show you in this section.

## Be precise with your niche

Before we move further into this section, we have to clear up two or three things. On the off chance that you need to take advantage of your visitor blogging attempts, at that point you have to ensure that the site which you have chosen to visitor present on is connected on your specialty. It can't be "kind of" related with your specialty, it must be unequivocally identified with your specialty.

For example, in the event that your specialty is tied in with weight training, at that point you discover a yoga site searching for a visitor blogger, don't proceed to attempt and post on their website as you won't increase any traffic from it. Kindly remember this progression as it is basic for your achievement in the blogging scene. You won't win any new readers from it. On the off chance that the "kind of" related site chooses to post your article on their site, they may lose a few readers and you may likewise lose a ton of regard in the blogging scene.

**Discovering sites to post on**

Before you feel free to discover locales to post on, ensure that the site you find is progressing nicely. The most ideal approach to see whether the sites are getting a ton of connected readers is to perceive what number of social offers a particular article or the site is getting.

That is a standout amongst the most ideal approaches to see whether the site is a go-go or no-go. Beyond any doubt you can post it on every one of the spots conceivable yet this will just make you look frantic for traffic That isn't what you need to look like in case you will have a long haul continued business. Presently there are a great deal of approaches to discover sites to post on, however the best site is clearly Google.

Simply look "Present a visitor post." If you see a site in your specialty which is tolerating visitor posts, email them. It is as basic as it sounds. They may request that you send a connection to your ongoing post so ensure you are composing the most ideal articles.

## Composing the post

When you at long last found your site to post your blog on and they have acknowledged you, it will be a great opportunity to compose the article. Contingent upon the webpage and their readers, your composing must be at a similar dimension as the site you will be visitor blogging on. This will enable you to pull in more readers to your blog.

So as to do that, you have to do explore about their site. Peruse every one of the articles you can on their site. At that point make sense of if their perusers are propelled level, apprentices or transitional. Since that will have a major effect in the rush hour gridlock, you will create from your visitor post.

You would prefer not to compose a careful article on a learner's site. It will just make readers neglect your articles. Generally speaking ensure that you are obliging their gathering of people. Which means, you need to compose a fundamental article if their site is an essential site and the other way around.

## Discover what is working

When you are doing your examination on the site, attempt to discover the most shared and the most seen post. That will enable you to make sense of what the group of onlookers needs. Attempt and compose a comparative post simply like the most prevalent one on their site. That will fulfill the site as they would get a great deal of perspectives and offers. Likewise, this will help you hugely support your blog subsequently developing your business.

Keep in mind, when you have the chance to compose on another person's blog, it isn't about you or your image. You are composing as a visitor, helping the site get more perspectives and offers. Visitor blogging will enable you to produce more traffic to your blog, however that ought not be your essential core interest.

In the event that you attempt and advance yourself in the visitor post, at that point odds of you landing more positions later on will be practically nothing. Trust me, you will get traffic from visitor posting yet don't advance yourself on the article.

By now you should have your product listing page built and your products on the way to the fulfillment center or waiting there ready to be sold! In this section I will be covering the most effective ways that you can start driving traffic to your product to make your initial sales. It's time to start making money!

# CHAPTER 10

# Best Tips & Tricks For A Succesful Business On Amazon

Free inventory from your house: In my house, and likely yours as well, there are those items that you have not been used, ever! Not since you bought it because it was on sale, or there was a discount on the commodity. You could have used it once and return to the furthest corner of your closet or kitchen cabinet; no matter the case, these items can be turned into cash or better, profit! All you have to do is ship them to Amazon for that to happen.

Go hunting! Look through your book shelves, not all books in your library you like them, get them out and create space for the series you have been dying to read in your house and also reduce clutter. Go into your cabinets in your kitchen, your kids (if you have any) rooms with their permission, of course, your room as well and get rid of anything that you do not use at all. Some items you can get will surprise you; as these items can be used to create profits on Amazon.

Take the initiative and involve your family, friends, and neighbor-if they are willing to do so-and use all these items to earn cash! It can be an excellent way to spend a weekend, go through your trash to make money.

Using dunnage for shipments: The stuff, either puffy or protective wrapper, which you use to wrap your load to protect them from touching the sides of your shipping box that is the definition of dunnage.

There are various things you can use to protect your items so that they can arrive safely to your customer without breakage. The commodities in the list below are things you are most likely going to have in your house already. You can use:

- A newspaper blanket
- A variety of small cardboard boxes for glass items
- From your online arbitrage purchases, you can use the air pillows in them
- Tie printed papers in your everyday plastic grocery bags. This is to protect your shipment from getting in contact with the newsprint.

Free boxes from grocery stores for shipment: At the beginning of your Amazon FBA business, there won't be the need for you to pay for delivery boxes as you might not have the cash for it or you want to save the money you have for something else. You can get shipping boxes for free from grocery stores, your neighbors who have moved recently, or your friends or colleagues that have moved as well as places that recycle their old boxes. This will save you tons of cash. Make sure you select the best boxes out of all those that are at your disposal.

From the grocery store, ask the employees or attendees when they are restocking their shelves if you can have some of the boxes they are using. They are likely to let you come and collect to your heart's content or even when they are restocking come and get the boxes from their aisles.

Lighter fluid to remove price stickers: When reusing shipment boxes, there is the likelihood of price stickers being on them. Removing them is one struggle you will have to endure if you are trying to save money, but getting rid of the sticker residue is another struggle all on its own. When it comes to dealing with the residue from price stickers lighter fluid will do the trick every time.

Be careful when handling the liquid, and this will guarantee the removal of the residue. The process is quite simple, and all you will require is a Scotty peeler to remove the labels. You can use a Ronsonol lighter fluid. To do this, you will:

- Pour some of the lighter fluid on the sticker residue you want to get rid off
- Wait for a few minutes, approximately 5 minutes before you can try and remove the labels
- Using your Scotty peeler, gently try and pry the tag off.

Free inventory from Freecycle.org: Join a group of your area on Freecycle Network to be able to see what people are getting rid of or giving away for free that you can use for your shipments. You might be shocked by the number of things that you can source using this network. I got board games- both used and new-; books, in boxes; kitchen appliances, among other things.

**The way it works is:**

- Claim an item on the Freecycle Network
- The owner will leave it on the front porch or sidewalk
- Go and collect your item!

And that's it! Fairly easy and straightforward. This makes it easy for you to coordinate with the owner as you will get to set a time that you will pass by to collect it.

Boxes from arbitrage purchases: To be honest, most of the sourcing that you do for this type of business is through online sourcing. This means that there will be shipments sent to you in boxes. Thus you can use these same boxes for your shipments to Amazon. But you have to go to be careful and remove all bar codes. This can be removed or covered up before you can use the UPS label or Amazon.

Productivity tools: There are times when you just need to have a nap without worrying over unnecessarily about the way your online store is doing or how the shipments are fairing or remember if you sent a reply to your customer's comment. Below are some productivity tools that can help you shave off some of that time:

- IFTTT (If This Then That): This is mainly used by sellers on Amazon or eBay. The app is used to alert the sellers of when sales have been made, or stock has been added back into inventory, or it has been added elsewhere.
- Facebook News Eradicator: With various sellers mainly spending their time on this social media platform going

through the different FBA groups, it can take much of your time without you realizing it. To help you with this, this eradicator cuts down your extension extremely low. It allows you not to spend so much time on the internet getting to know what all your sources on Amazon FBA are talking about or all seller community groups.

- Cleer Pro: is an online app for online arbitrage. It is a software that makes it easier for you as a vendor to browse easily when trying to look for deals, items or doing your research on Amazon.com

- Gmail Canned Responses: typing a similar response over and over again can get exhausting, and no one wants that kind of stress. Therefore, this app allows you to formulate a response that is going to reply automatically to the type of replies that come from your customers. The same app can be used to respond to an email you get in your Amazon seller inbox. Since Amazon allows you to use your email to respond to customers instead of creating a particular kind of email address, you can use this app.

- Flashback Express: it can only be used on Windows, unfortunately. It can be used to quickly capture and annotate your voice and then upload the video on your screen. This can be used to communicate something that is in your store. Or deliver something that is on your screen to a colleague or your occasional customer. This makes the message more personal than ever, and it can be the best way to explain something to your customers in an easier manner, and it can make you quite popular among other clients. It can bring you more customers as well.

- Unroll.me: There are dozens upon dozens of emails that you receive from a seller on a daily basis about different offers that you are going to get from Amazon. The difference between having this app and not having it, is you are required to need to keep clicking delete or unsubscribe manually. This app allows you to unsubscribe from those emails or offers that you do not want to have in bulk. There are tutorials online that you can use to help you navigate through the app with ease.

Time saving hacks: To save your time as a salesperson when screening your items and scanning them, you can use the $0.00 buy cost to help you when browsing for items mainly in the app's field "Buy$." The time that you spend typing at the expense of the item is deducted since it costs nothing! You can use a calculator to subtract the actual buying price of the item from the profit price and decide on whether you will purchase the item or you will forgo it.

At times, it is not necessary for you to do the math of whether you will get to buy the product; all you have got to do is check if the price you are buying the item is higher or lower than the price of the profit you are bound to make.

An example would be if the cost of the head gear is at $12.99 and the profit you are required to make is at $9.99; you will not buy the item since it costs more than what you are going to get from the profit.

Other ways of reducing the scanning process are through downloading the Amazon 1Button app. It is an extension from chrome that shows you the price of the item you require, and it does the searching or looking or scanning for you.

An instance would be when looking for game boards; the app will let you know if the game is sold on Amazon and the price of the game. This saves you the trouble of going through Amazon trying to find the game and if it is even available and the price as well.

Keep in mind that not always does the search engine provide the results that you are looking for and at times the items might not even be available or found.

Make sure you invest in the best supplies you possibly can get your hands on. There are the common denominators of supplies that most Amazon sellers have in their arsenal and use them. Most of them swear by these items and can attest to their immense help when carrying out their daily sales.

Have a business credit card and checking account: in your daily life, you have a personal credit card that you use mainly to buy your items and spend it as you wish. You also, most definitely (if not, get one ASAP!) keep track of your expenses and savings as well.

You can have a software tracking app on your every expense charged to your credit card, be it personal or business. For the Amazon FBA, you need to have a business credit card and checking account to keep track of what you are spending on and where your money goes. This card and account need to be different from your credit and checking account.

You can use Quickbooks as a way to keep track of your personal and business accounts and credit cards. The app allows you to:

- Keep track of what you have spent
- Know how much you owe your credit card and
- Where you shop at

Run your business like a business: With this being your business, even if you are running it at your house, you need to run it like one. To make shipping easier, create your shipping and prepping station.

It doesn't have to be anything fancy or too elaborate, get a small table and lean it against a wall. Have drawers (they could be colored or whatever pattern you prefer) close by that house all your poly bags, shipping tapes, scissors, liquid fluid and any other necessary appliance that you need to wrap your shipping items and put them in your box.

Having or creating order in your house can help you run your business very smoothly. The station will help you reduce the time spent running around looking for scissors, the shipping tape or trying to figure out where to lay your merchandise at so that you can work.

The area around your working station can function as your prepping station, where you gather all your necessary items, put them together before you move to your working station to put the final touches on your product before shipping them off to your customer.

The station can act as a studio of some sort. When you have laid out your items on the table, you can take a picture of the items and use them for your store on Amazon. The pictures can be edited; changing the color in the background to pure white t put it on the product listing images section of your site. You can learn more on how on Photoshop Elements on this site http://www.secondhalfdreams.com/4202/how-to-create-an-image-that-meets-amazons-requirements/

Know a good deal when you see one: While finding a niche is important to the long-term strength of your FBA store, the most important rule of FBA is that if you can make a profit on it then you should sell it. As such, regardless of what the product is if you find yourself staring at a sale that is 75 percent off or more then there is always going to be room enough there for you to make a profit on the item. The key to not putting too much work into this type of passive income is to always passively be on the lookout for good deals and be ready and able to jump on them when you see them because the best deals are never going to stick around for very long.

Care about your seller rating: Just because you letting Amazon do most of the heavy lifting doesn't mean that you can let your store run on autopilot. Specifically, you are going to want to be aware of your seller rating and do everything you can to keep it as high as possible. If you sell faulty merchandise or items that fall apart quickly then this number will drop rapidly which means you will want to consider all the costs of a particular product, not just what you pay to take direct ownership of the product.

# CHAPTER 11

# The Most Important Things to Grow Your Amazon Business

Growing your Amazon business requires you to not only start it and create a successful first launch, but also to maintain it and continue growing it every single day. As you already know, you are going to be required to launch multiple products and continue to build buzz around your business, if you are going to generate any level of success. The more that you can increase awareness around your business and grow your business out, the more sales you are going to make and, in turn, the more profits you will make as well. This way, you can create maximum sales through your business, which will allow you to earn even more over time.

Many people think that growing your business means that you will have to put in even more work to keep your business running, but the truth is that you can grow your business and still keep it highly passive, if you want to. The key is to automate wherever you can, so that you can leverage more platforms and strategies without having to use up too much more of your time. In addition to automation, you want to stay consistent in your strategies and stick to what you know. This way, running your business stays easy and you continue to produce the same great results that you have already been producing all along.

In this chapter, we are going to discuss how you can grow your business without massively increasing your workload. This way, you can improve your profits, increase your revenue, and create an even stronger income through Amazon FBA without taking up too much more of your time.

## Stay Consistent, Use What Works

When it comes to growing your Amazon FBA business, you want to use what works and remain consistent in how you approach your business. Consistency provides benefits to your business in many different ways, including in ways that directly influence both you and your customer. The impacts that consistency has on both parties is important, as it makes running your business easier, and it makes relying on your business and trusting in your quality of products and services easier.

Regarding yourself and your business, remaining consistent makes running your business easier because you already know what you are doing. As you repeat the same launch processes and growth strategies repeatedly, you will find that despite some of the details changing, the consistency in the strategy makes generating success a breeze. With consistency in this area, you prevent yourself from having to completely design new strategies from scratch every single time you want to launch a new product or market in a new way. This way, rather than starting from scratch, you can improve on the practices that you have already been using and continue to refine and evolve your tried and true practices over time. In the end, this is going to make running your business much easier and will contribute to your success in both maintaining and growing your business over the years.

With your audience, consistency gives them something to rely on and trust in. When your audience sees you using the same launch strategies repeatedly, they are more likely to trust in what you have to offer because they come to know your strategies, too. As they see, your strategies put into action repeatedly, it cultivates a consistent image in their minds of who you are and what you have to offer. This leaves no room for confusion or overwhelm, and ensures that there is no reason for your customers to think that you do not have a clear sense of direction with what you are doing. Instead, they see you using your consistent approach and they recognize it as being your style and personality thrown into your brand, effectively marketing your business. In other words, your consistency becomes a part of your image and actually improves your brand loyalty.

Companies that are known to change their approaches too frequently often destroy their momentum and lose their audience's attention and loyalty because no one can keep up with what they are doing. Their customers grow confused with the way things work, are unaware of what is going on with the business at any given time, and do not feel confident in the company or the way that they do business. The company's inability to commit to any given strategy often comes across as being flaky or unreliable, which can massively reduce the quality of their reputation. In the end, it pays to be predictable and repetitive in your approach, and keep your customers developing curiosity through the details.

## Extend Your Online Presence

Social media is a powerhouse when it comes to marketing, no matter what you are marketing for. If you want to grow your brand awareness and increase your traffic to your website, using social media is a great opportunity for you to do so. In fact, when you have to grow your business on Amazon FBA and get more traffic into your store, social media is actually a key player.

Extending your online presence essentially means that you put more effort into being active and engaged on multiple platforms, while also leveraging the strategies available on those platforms to help you grow. For example, if you are presently using Instagram and Facebook to market your products, you could extend your online presence by using Twitter, YouTube, and even Pinterest or LinkedIn to begin marketing your products to your target audience. When you do extend your online presence, make sure that you are extending into platforms where your audience actually spends time, so that you are more likely to get right in front of them. This way, you are making the extension of your presence worthwhile, which will ultimately help you grow your business rapidly with social media.

As you do extend your presence, you want to take advantage of the services that each platform has to offer when it comes to marketing. You can also take advantage of marketing automation to ensure that your platforms stay active and engaged, even when you are not presently using them. This is a great way to keep your platforms passive while still earning you a greater presence and income.

Concerning leveraging marketing tools on social media, one of the biggest features you should focus on is native advertising. Native advertisements are paid promotions that exist directly on any given social media platform, and that often fall in line with their newsfeed so that they see it amongst their existing posts. When it comes to growing your presence, these native advertisements can offer you the same benefits that AMS advertisements offer you, further extending your reach without much effort on your behalf. Including native advertisements on social media platforms as a part of your ad budget, is a great opportunity to reach even more people and drive even more traffic to your Amazon store, further improving your sales reach.

## Automate Wherever You Can

When it comes to growing your business while still maintaining the passive element of it, it pays to automate whenever and wherever you can. Automation is a powerful tool that can help you stay active on social media, or any other platform, without actually having to physically log on and partake in activities on that platform on a regular basis. Running your business through automation earns you time freedom while your business still stays active enough to earn you an income, which earns you financial freedom, too.

For advertisements, the automation ultimately comes from paying them to exist, and then only needing to check in on them once per week to make sure that they are still performing properly and earning you a strong income. These are one of the best ways to run automation, as they guarantee you some form of attention to your advertisements and help you grow your business rapidly and successfully.

Another automation feature that you can use is accomplished by using a platform like HootSuite or HubSpot. These platforms allow you to log in to all of your social media accounts on one single platform, then create, and schedule posts for those platforms ahead of time. For many of them, you can create a single post and have it sent out to multiple different social media platforms in a single go, maximizing the use of that particular post and making it easier for you to be found online. When you do get started using automation platforms, make sure that you automate no further than one to two weeks in advance, as automating too far in advance can leave you with outdated marketing materials, should you find that trends change and your materials are all geared toward outdated trends. Moreover, checking in weekly or bi-weekly helps you monitor analytics and ensure that your posts are getting excellent results, improving your chances at growing your presence on these platforms more consistently and rapidly.

## The Value of Momentum

Momentum, as you know, is a valuable tool to have in place when we talk about launching new products and earning sales with new product lines. That being said, momentum is not exclusive to new product launches when it comes to growing your business. If you want to grow your Amazon FBA business consistently, you want to make sure that you are leveraging momentum in every way possible with your business. The best way to do this is to make sure that you are paying attention to every opportunity that you are receiving with your business, and to take advantage of as many of them as you possibly can. The more opportunities that you take advantage of, the more times you are going to get your business seen by a new audience and the more sales that you are going to make overall. This is crucial if you want to be successful with Amazon FBA, so it is important that you be always on the lookout or in the process of making new opportunities for yourself to take.

When you do take up these new opportunities, do not rely on them exclusively to build your momentum. Instead, leverage them in every way possible so that you can maximize the amount of momentum that you are gaining from each opportunity. This way, not only you are getting direct benefits from the opportunities themselves, but you are also getting benefits from talking about these opportunities and building your audience's excitement in them, too. The more that you can combine new opportunities by talking about new opportunities, the more momentum you are going to continue to grow in your business, which will lead to increased success.

You can track your momentum by paying attention to your analytics. If at any point you find your business is not growing the way you desire it to, chances are you can find the exact problem directly in your analytics. Below, we will discuss the value of your analytics and how you can use them to guide your business forward.

## Use Your Analytics to Guide You

As I have mentioned throughout this book, your analytics are a powerful source of data that can directly tell you what your audience may not be willing to say aloud. When you use your analytics to guide you, you can feel confident that you are directly listening to what your audience wants more of an offer more of what they are looking for. This way, as you continue to share new pieces of marketing materials with your audience, you can feel confident that every single piece is going to succeed with reaching your audience and generating success for your business.

In the matter of reading your analytics, there is a simple system for reading them to ensure that your posts are gaining traction. First, you want to see how many people saw the post, and then you want to see how many people engaged with the post. Ideally, you want to have at least a 2-8% or higher engagement ratio, as this tends to be a standard ratio on most platforms. You might have some pieces of content that perform at 30% + engagement ratios and others that perform lower than 2%. Naturally, you want to look at each piece of content and start seeing what the differences are, in order to begin to understand why some contents perform well, and why other contents do not.

If you look at the content that thrives versus the content that struggles, you should be able to identify some obvious differences or patterns that highlight why some products work and why others do not. You might notice nuances as if your underperforming content has lower quality graphics or graphics that all feature similar content that, for some reason or another, does not seem to resonate well with your audience. Or, you might find that there are certain topics that you are talking about in either that is causing your audience to like or ignore the content that you have created. As you notice these patterns, jot them down and keep track of them, as this is going to help you understand your audience better.

Ideally, you should be reading your analytics every single week, especially right before you begin to create new content for your platforms. Reading your analytics before creating new content can help you create new content that is actually relevant to what your audience wants to see and read about. This way, you are more likely to create new content that performs even better than previous content.

The more that you create higher quality, relevant content for your audience, the more you are going to recognize your positive momentum growing in your favor and helping you expand your business reach. This will help your analytic tracking work together with leveraging your momentum to help you grow your business and earn more sales over time.

## Build Out Your Product Line

The final and perhaps most obvious way for you to grow your Amazon FBA business is to continually add new products to your product line. After your initial launch with all of your new products in your new store, you want to start adding new products to your shop on a consistent basis. The key to building out your product line is that you want to be consistent, but not overwhelming. This way, you are going to have plenty to talk about and grow into, without bombarding your audience with constant back-to-back launches, which can be overwhelming and can actually drive your audience away. Although they do want to see that you are growing and adding new options or products for them to order, they do not want to constantly hear from you with your new offerings, as this may desensitize them and cause them to ignore your new launches.

Most successful companies choose to launch a new lineup of products every 3 months or every quarter. This gives them an entire quarter to devote to choosing these new products, organizing the launch, and conducting the launch, then conducting the launch follow up and then to grow momentum in between with standard marketing practices. If you choose to do this, you can perfect a 3-month marketing strategy complete with all of the aforementioned marketing cycles for every new product lineup that you add to your business. This way, you always know what you are marketing for and you have an easy time-sharing your new products with your audience.

If you do choose to build out your product line with lineups like this every three months, it is important that you slightly alter your product research phase to look for products that are likely going to be popular for the next season. After all, you do not want to be marketing for last season's products in the new season when you do each new marketing launch. For example, you do not want to be marketing cozy sweaters or Christmas gift items in the spring when you start your new launch cycles. Make sure that you are always being realistic about what is popular now and what is likely to remain popular come your launch cycle, so that you are stocking up on products that are more likely to sell.

The alternative to doing quarterly launches is to launch a new product every month or every other month. This way, your launch cycle would look more like spending 1-2 weeks in the launch phase, launching a new product, and spending 1-2 weeks in follow up phase as you build on the momentum of that new product. By the time, that product has been out for a couple of weeks, you can start preparing for the launch of your next product. This style of marketing is like taking baby steps with your momentum by growing it out consistently over time, without ever really taking a beat between your marketing strategies.

If you do choose to market this way, make sure that you take periodic breaks in between your launches to give your audience a chance to take a break, too. Remember: your audience is not going to want to buy something new from you every single month as they have other things they want to purchase, too. Unless you have a massive audience that cycles between who buys each month, you are going to generate your best success this way by launching a new product every 6-8 weeks, so that there is plenty of time between each launch for your audience to recover and prepare for a new launch.

# CHAPTER 12

# Managing Fba Inventory

If you want to stay in a seller relationship with Amazon, you need to make sure that you always have enough inventories on your hands to cover customer demand. However, when using the Fulfillment by Amazon service it may be hard to keep track of this, as the products are no longer in plain sight.

In the "Manage Inventory" page there is a suite of tools that allow almost real-time management of your inventories, and it is really important that you learn how to use and squeeze the most out of each one of them.

### a) All Inventory View

This is one of the three main pages that you will find in the "Manage Inventory" portion of the seller central. You will use this page to create new listings and offer your products on Amazon. In here you will also find all the listings you have created on Amazon.

Once the listing is created, you need to select the box that appears at the left of it and use the "actions" dropdown menu to convert the order processing method to Fulfilled by Amazon. You can also do the same process backward to change it back to Fulfilled by Merchant in the case you want to handle a particular product.

## b) Inventory Amazon Fulfills

On this page, you will find all the information regarding the listings that Amazon fulfills for you. Data like the merchant SKU, the title, condition, price and quantity of your products are displayed on sortable tables.

At the bottom of the screen, you will find four tabs that provide you with a wealth of information related to shipped products. Whether they are inbound (seller to Amazon) or Outbound (Amazon to the customer) you will find all the information you need.

The first tab is the Summary, where you will find the following information.

- Inbound: The quantity of every shipment that has not yet been received by Amazon.
- Fulfillable: This shows the number of products within the network that Amazon will be able to pick, pack and ship.
- Unfulfillable: This shows the number of products that Amazon has deemed unfit for sale.
- Reserved: This refers to your products within the network that is currently tied to order or are moving between centers.
- MFN Listing: If it says "Yes" the item is listed for fulfillment by Merchant.
- AFN Listing: A "yes" here indicates Amazon lists the item for fulfillment.

The second tab is called "Inbound" and it has information regarding all the shipments you have done to an Amazon fulfillment center.

- Working quantity refers to shipments you already notified Amazon about.

- Inbound quantity is the number of shipments you provided a tracking number for.

- Receiving quantity is the number of shipments that already reached the fulfillment center and are being processed.

- Inbound problem quantity refers to the items that reached the center but can't be processed due to any reason.

- Total inbound quantity is the summary of all the above numbers.

The Outbound tab provides you with information regarding the inventory that has been shipped to a customer. Here you will find the date and type of shipment, the quantity of the product and the shipping price.

The last tab is the "Events" tab, where you can check all the events related to your products that Amazon fulfills. It shows you the date the event occurred, the type of event (Receipt, outbound shipment, and adjustment) and the number of products involved in the event.

### c) The Shipping Queue

On the last part of the Manage Inventory Page, you will find all the information regarding your shipments to Amazon fulfillment centers.

It is also the page you use to notify Amazon of your shipments, editing a shipment and deleting or canceling one of them.

The shipment status will tell you where your products stand in the shipping workflow and it is on this screen where you can make most of the actions related to your shipments. Below are the names of the status that you can find on this page.

- Working: There is information you haven't inputted yet.
- Ready to ship: The information is complete, but you haven't marked the item shipped yet.
- Shipped: This means you clicked the "mark as shipped" button for the products.
- In-Transit: This only applies to FTL and LTL shipments, and it indicates that there is an appointment made for delivery.
- Delivered: The carrier has indicated they delivered the shipment.
- Checked-In: The center reported the delivery.
- Directed to Prep: The order has been directed to the prep center for the appropriate labeling and preparation.
- Receiving: The contents are being scanned and added to your inventory.
- Closed: All the contents of your shipment have been processed and are ready for fulfillment.
- Canceled: You have canceled the shipment.
- Deleted: You have deleted the shipment.

- Receiving w/ problems: There were problems found in your shipment.

On this page, you can also edit any shipment that hasn't been received in a fulfillment center. It is possible to set up a notification system that will let you know via e-mail when your products get checked-in. When they are being processed into the inventory of a fulfillment center and when the process is completed.

### d) Tools for Managing FBA Inventory

If you find the suite of tools provided by Amazon insufficient to manage your inventories, you may want to try a third-party app. There are many of these apps in the market, and you will have to do some research to find the one that suits your needs the best.

### 1 - Ecomdash

Ecomdash, for example, is a tool that focuses on making it easier for you to manage your inventories across multiple platforms. When it comes to the world of internet selling, your inventory is the most important part of your business, as people who buy online don't want to wait a long time to receive their products.

Most of the tools you will find out there has this focus, to make it easier for you to work on many different platforms and marketplaces. It is recommended that you invest in one of these tools once your business starts expanding, as you will need a hand to stay organized and make sure you don't disregard any platform you work on.

## 2 - Teikametrics

Another useful tool is called teikametrics. This app offers a huge amount of information and statistics about sales. It is built to help you maximize your profits on Amazon. You can find graphs on everything, from seasonal trends to the most sold items.

It also helps you make your inventory efficient and profitable. You can track what are the items that sell the most in your inventories, compare the profit made from your items of different brands, you can use this info to prioritize these products and make the most out of your FBA membership.

This tool can also help you take a systematic and efficient approach to stale inventory. One of the disadvantages of FBA is that since you don't see the products all the time you don't really notice if your inventory is going stale. Stale inventory can be a waste of space and it will produce extra FBA fees if it sleeps in storage for too long.

The important part about third-party tools is that they need to offer you something you're lacking. Really think about the needs you have as a seller, and if Amazon is not giving you all you need to be successful then don't be afraid to look somewhere else to enhance your experience and your profit.

# CHAPTER 13

# How To Do Marketing Like An Expert Without Knowing Anything

You already got brief information about what marketing is. Now, I will tell you how to do and set up a marketing strategy. You've gone through the internet and you have a product or a service and you've been trying to find information to market that product or service online effectively. You just have no idea where to start. You may know some of the fundamental principles but I want to take you through the beginning stages step by step.

Some of the things you need to keep in mind when first starting to market your business on the internet fundamentally online marketing are really simple. It's all about generating leads and converting those leads into sales. Let me break that down a little bit. So, what exactly do I mean by generating leads?

A lead is basically the contact information of your potential or ideal customer. For example, this can be a name and an email address, email address, a phone number or this might be a postal address. Nine times out of ten when doing online marketing the least information that you ask from a person, the more likely they are to give it to you. So, an email address is normally quite sufficient. And once you have the contact information of your potential customer, then you have to think about converting.

Which basically means turning that person from just being a lead or just being a piece of contact information to actually becoming a customer of yours. Now that's easier to do once you have their information because you can contact them via email or phone number or whatever contact information that you took from them. And you can use that information to sell to them. In terms of online marketing, email is still one of the best resources in terms of converting a lead into a sale.

If you're not using email marketing, potentially you're missing out on huge sales to your product or your service online. The second thing that sells the most is a funnel. Now you should be thinking about funnel before you even create your website before you even start on social media or send in traffic to your website. The fundamental medium to sell is your sales funnel. Basically, the sales funnel is the process that you take someone through from becoming a visitor on your website all the way to becoming one of your paying clients.

Now there are four stages in a basic sales funnel, the first stage is to have what is known as a lead magnet. This is something of value that you can give away for free in return for that person's name or email address or contact information which is important for your business. Now you want to keep in mind you don't really want to ask for someone's phone number unless it's directly linked with whatever it is that your business is about.

For example, if your lead magnet or what you're giving away for free is a telephone coaching, which is probably really rare for you to do. But let's just say it is a telephone coaching. In that scenario, it would be okay to ask for someone's phone number. However, nine times out of ten give someone a PDF or a downloadable or an e-book or an e-guide or video course is normally sufficient as a lead magnet.

So, an example of a great lead magnet, let's say you sell clothes for babies on your website or on Amazon FBA. You might have a lead magnet maybe a free guide on parenting tips or tips for newborn babies.

The third thing to do effective marketing is traffic. The age-old saying is "traffic plus conversions equals its sales". Now, this is a formula that I want you to keep in mind. A lot of people are way too focused on traffic and how many visitors they get into any particular website or web page, or how many visitors they get into their store. When in reality it doesn't really matter necessarily how many people you can get to a page but it matters how many people you can convert from being a visitor to a lead or a sale on that page. So, you should be thinking about both not just about traffic, but also how well is your web page going to convert.

Finally, I want to emphasize content marketing. Why it's important to think about content marketing and have a content marketing strategy in place while marketing your product or service online. So, content marketing is basically is using the content as a way to market your product or your service online. When you have a website, you want your website to be full of rich content that attracts your target customers to your website.

Let's go back to the example of selling baby clothes. If you have a lot of tips for mothers and for parents about parenting or about the types of things to keep in mind when having a newborn child, and if you have lots of information on your website for mothers and for fathers. The parents can come to your site for really useful information, then your website becomes a hub for your target customers to come and to get information. And obviously, you've also got products and services on your website that will help that customer base even further.

One more important factor in marketing is social media marketing. People just love to visit these mediums to see which product or business has better reviews than others. There is a trust factor associated with social media. Products or business that surpasses the expectations of their customers has a better reputation on social media. You can't ignore social media websites like Facebook, Twitter, YouTube, Pinterest, LinkedIn, and more.

Pay Per Click is another main thing to understand when you are starting with the marketing of your products. If you have just started then it may be difficult for you to get customers to buy your products. You can place your ads, on the relevant pages. Whenever a customer will search for a product related to yours, an ad will be shown to them. By visiting that link the customer will be able to buy your product. This type of marketing is paid but can be worthwhile if done right.

These were just a few tips to help you market your product or your service online. If you want to successfully use these marketing methods, then you must have a marketing strategy, to begin with. Your success depends upon this strategy and the way you apply this strategy.

**How to apply the strategy?**

1. Know your customers - This is the first step to establish any marketing strategy. You just have to know your customers. What are their needs and problems, and how can you or your product help them? Create surveys or social media campaigns. Where you post relevant things and customers can interact with you through comments and messages.

2. Find out what steps your customers need to take - When you have figured out who you want to sell, now find out what you want your customers to do next. For example, you want them to buy your products. But you must walk them through this stage. To do this, you can create an email list or a social media page where your customers can find out about the new products you are launching.

3. Use funnels - Your customers will take the exact step you want them to take if you will use funnels. You can create content that drives the customers from the discovery into consideration and then purchase stage. The most prominent methods to create funnels is to write blogs, social media posts, emails, and ads.

If you are not willing to do all of these activities on your own, then hire a freelancer online. A freelancer is a professional that works for your business in exchange for money. You can hire any freelancer around the world.

There are many reputed freelancing platforms including Upwork, Freelancer, Fiverr, People Per Hour, and more!

## 2. How to Destroy Your Competitors

There are many ways to destroy your competitors. If you want to completely dominate your amazon niche and you want to win as an online seller, then continue reading the next steps. It is the fact that most of the sellers on Amazon have no idea what they're doing. They're not doing what they are supposed to be doing to become successful on Amazon. They don't put any effort into their listings.

They're literally just throwing up products on Amazon from China. They just copy and pasting descriptions from Alibaba onto Amazon and they're making a decent income. If you will check the trends on Jungle Scout or any other tools that I have mentioned earlier, you will know what I am talking about. But this is not how you can earn consistently on Amazon. To dominate such insane competition, you should follow the steps as explained below:

1.  **Reviews** - Never neglect reviews. When you sell something online, reviews are really important. I would say that the reviews are probably the most important decision factor that people take in when they're buying a product on Amazon. So, you need to have amazing reviews. For your first 10 reviews, you're going to have to hustle to get them. They're not just

going to magically appear. Until you have your first 10 reviews nobody's really going to buy your product. Because people don't want to be the first to try something out. People always want social proof. So how do you get these reviews? Go on Facebook review groups and offer the product for free in exchange for a PayPal refund on the purchase. If you don't want to refund them on PayPal you can also offer them 97 percent off coupon codes. However, you will not be verified as soon as you use a coupon code. This is so important by the way as soon as I use a coupon code for a review it won't be shown as a verified review. Amazon is just going to make it an unverified review that still appears on your listing. But they carry no weight as much as a verified review. Make sure that you get verified reviews and the way to do that is through Facebook review groups. Keep searching FBA deals and reviews and Club Amazon reviews or any group that is available for your country. You'll find a ton of review groups. Any review groups that have over five thousand people join them and usually update requests to join them and then just post your product in there. Offer a PayPal refund in exchange for the review that way the review will be verified. Obviously, the person has to wait for the product to come and then they can review it. The beautiful thing about this is you can actually talk to the reviewer that is going to get to review your product. You can ask them to actually include a picture in their reviews because reviews with pictures carry the most weight.

2. **Combination** - The second-best way to dominate your competitors is bundling. If there's clearly an opportunity to bundle a product with another product that your customers want together, and it's not being offered. Obviously, it can be an amazing way to destroy everybody in your niche. Because you're offering a unique selling proposition. So, you're offering your own little spin on the product and that's all of the entrepreneurship. You literally copy what works and you just put your own little spin on it. That's what entrepreneurship is. You don't need to come up with some next-level ideas. As we've been taught, you don't need to have some great idea, you can just copy what works. And then you put your own little spin on it to differentiate it just slightly. The beauty is even if you don't differentiate on Amazon, you still make money. It's such a diverse market. If you click on a product that you're thinking of selling and you scroll down and it says "customers who bought this also bought that." This is the golden section right there where you will find another product to bundle together. The beautiful thing about bundling is that you can actually offer a higher price point than the rest of these sellers. So, for example, if your niche is at a low price point and everybody's selling for 11 or 12 dollars. You can sell both together and sell it for $20. Now you have a healthy profit margin. It might cost you an extra dollar to source the second thing. This stuff is cheap if you source it from China. How you actually bundle it and ship it into Amazon? You have to find the two suppliers that make both of the products. Or get one

product from the first supplier who manufactures everything. Put your logo on it and then ship it to the second supplier. So, you have to communicate with the supplier. The second supplier puts it together and makes sure that when the product reaches Amazon, it's already packaged the way that your customers are going to receive it. Remember that Amazon is not going to repackage your thing. They're literally going to take what they got in the warehouse and they're going to send it out. They're not going to do anything else other than just take it and hold it in the warehouse.

3. **Bullet Points** - The fifth way to absolutely destroy the competitors is having amazing bullet points and amazing descriptions. When a customer reads them you literally put yourself in the shoes of your target market and you basically write what they want to hear. As soon as a customer starts reading the bullet points and they're literally hypnotizing. They start wanting to buy it right away. And the second thing is having a captivating description. So, you basically use some HTML. It's not very hard to do so. You can learn by searching on Google. Or you can outsource this task to a freelancer on Upwork.

4. **Pretty Pictures** - Yes, you heard it right. The very first way to destroy competitors is having beautiful pictures. This is super important. Obviously, pictures are the first thing that your customers see when they click on your listing and you obviously want the pictures to be amazing. Especially the first picture you want that to be something like this - as soon as the

customer sees your listing, they see the picture. And they're like "wow I want to buy this right away." Most of the listings on Amazon doesn't have a beautiful first picture. The first picture has to be on a white background and I recommend getting professional photos done if you're actually serious about building an Amazon business. If you're serious about building a brand, it's just going to pay off in the long run. Where do you get professional photos for Amazon FBA? Just find a local photographer on Craigslist there's a ton of college kids that need to get photography jobs. All of them mostly have fancy cameras. If no one is available locally, then you can find a photographer on Fiverr or Upwork. I'm sure that they can help you without charging a lot of money. Just pay them some money and tell them exactly what you want. Or find someone on Upwork or Fiverr. The pictures are of great importance and the pictures will cost between about 10 and 30 dollars. The best part about it is that you don't even need a lot of pictures. You only need four pictures. You can use non-professional pictures along with one or two professionally photographer pictures. And Photoshop the logo of your business to these pictures. If you don't know how to use Photoshop, you can again go to Fiverr and Upwork. You don't have to waste your time on things that you don't know how to do. You have to be spending your time productively on something that will give you a return on investment on your time. Do something that will actually make you money. The first picture like I said it needs to be a beautiful photo of the product on a white background. You also need a couple of action shots. For example, if the product is some kind of beauty product. Maybe it can be a beauty tool or something like a hairdryer. You need to have some pictures of a person using the product.

5. **Amazon Ads** - So the fourth best way to destroy competitors are having amazing PPC campaigns. Nobody really knows how to do PPC on Amazon and it's not that hard. The thing with PPC is that it's a step by step thing. You have to actually create the ads properly. You find a product, then you source it from Alibaba, then you make the listing, you get beautiful pictures and do all other things.

6. **Price** - You can compete or knock out your competitors by providing a price that is less than your competitors. Don't make the price too low though. The customer might think that you are selling a cheap or duplicate product.

# CHAPTER 14

# Grow - How To Move Forward?

Finally, you already have a profitable product, a good supplier and, a well-tested product to sell on Amazon. What needs to be done now is to go into details and see how far your business can grow and do it fulltime.

From the research and process you have done, try to evaluate and answer the following questions:

- How much money can I make?
- Which supplier would I like to deal with?
- How many units should my first bulk order be?

As your business grows, you'll be doing the same process from finding a product and suppliers to testing and selling the products. It may take time to gain sales volume if you'd compare it with other sales channels. Outgrowing other channels will still depend on the limitation of your supplier.

Also, the growth of your business is up to you, whether you want to make it small or big. Nonetheless, I want you to find ways on how to grow your Amazon selling by taking any possibilities that will make your sales increase. You can do this when you have enough capital for the inventory. After all, with the use of Amazon FBA to fulfill orders, you'll have more time to look for opportunities to grow your business.

Here are just a few suggestions to your online selling business while you sell on Amazon FBA:

## 1 - Create own sales channel

Having your own e-Commerce store can be an added venue to build your product line. You may want to build your own website as another sales channel.

## 2 - Sell more new products

The more good products you sell the more feedback you get. Make use of it to improve your product line. If supplier permits, you can ask them to customize any aspect of the product for you. If they do so, you may only be paying extra for the customization. It may be complicated, and so the terms and conditions with your supplier must be drafted accordingly.

## 3 - Brand yourself

Being an Amazon FBA seller makes you reputable as well and it would be easier to brand yourself according to your product lists. Review on how you would like to continue addressing the needs of your customers to come up with the best brand for you.

## 4 - Negotiate better prices from supplier

As your sales grow, your purchases likewise increase. By this time, your bargaining power over your suppliers must be fulfilled by asking small discounts on several orders to them. To do this, you should ensure that you're able to build a good relationship with your supplier.

## 5 - Establish recurring revenue

You'll make more money on your business when you're able to establish recurring revenue. Get into having some promotional items or start a monthly package and the like. You can also start an email newsletter from any contact databases you have.

When you start selling on Amazon, take advantage of all the tools that come along. Keeping yourself updated and proactive will bring your business to what you've been wishing for. Every successful seller starts with a small enterprise and the only reason they grow is because they are consistent and persistent at work.

## BECOMING A TOP SELLER IN AMAZON

As we've been discussing in this book. FBA is the best way to sell online. They will take the products you are going to sell, store, and ship it for you. You will not have to deal with any type of customer service either since they will handle all returns and exchanges. We've gone over the benefits of selling through Amazon using FBA and now we'll discuss strategies to become a top seller.

There's no guarantee that you will sell your products and make money automatically. This is why we'll need to have launch strategies that will put our products at the top of rankings when customers search for products. To summarize, the Amazon algorithm for ranking products is, the more sales and good reviews the products has then the higher its ranking will be on Amazon. A highly ranked product gets a lot of sales without the seller doing any work.

Giving away products is a great way to garner sales and positive reviews. Since customers are always looking for deals online make sure you set a very low price ($1-2) to get buyers' attention. This is a great way to rank up the list quickly. Amazon even has a function where you can set up promotions for a product and print out coupon claim codes. Give these coupons to your friends and family, have them order the product at a low price using the coupon and then ask them for their honest reviews.

The downside to this strategy is that it will be nearly impossible to make any profit. You may get as close to breaking even but that is only if your product is cheap to make. Therefore, I recommend starting with an inexpensive product first so you don't lose as much money while ranking up the lists.

Amazon Ads is the advertising feature on Amazon that allows sellers to get exposure for the products on the website. I recommend that every seller should be using Amazon Ads because it will lead to more sales, which will also rank your product higher. When first beginning with Amazon Ads we should start with the "Automatic" targeting system. This way you're ads will be spread around the website evenly. There's also a "Daily Budget" that is set to determine how much exposure your product receives. The higher the budget, the more advertisement you get for your product.

Once your product begins selling, head to the report section in Amazon Ads and search what keywords buyers are using when they search for your product. After identifying the words switch the targeting to "Manual" and enter those specific keywords.

There are certain websites designed for Amazon sellers that promote and sell your products on other people's list. This will spread your product to other online markets and gain even more exposure. There are fees however and usually, you will have to give away your product with coupons. This is not necessary but for many products they do help boost sales and reviews. I recommend websites such as Buview or Zonblast.

There are bloggers from all around the world who's hobby is to receive products, review them and if they enjoyed the item then they will happily advertise it on their Blog and share it with other bloggers. A popular website for this is Tomoson.com. All you have to do is set up an account for free and list your product. Bloggers will come flocking wanting to receive and promote your product.

As a requirement, you need to give away your product using $1 coupons. Once a member from Tomoson receives the product you have the option to have them either post a review on their Blog and then link to Amazon, put together a Youtube video review then linking it to Amazon, post it on their social media with a link to Amazon or to just leave an honest review on Amazon.

Most of the time this service is free but many popular Bloggers will charge you for this type of advertisement. The range could be from $10 all the way to $50. However, if the Blogger is popular enough with many followers then spending this extra money can generate a lot of sales.

The key to becoming a top seller is not maximizing profit at first but to generate sales and good reviews. Giving your products away using Amazon coupons to people who will generate good reviews for your products does this. Once our item is high in the rankings then it will sell on its own.

One of the easiest ways to sell more on Amazon is to raise the ranking of your products. This has a lot of advantages and will increase your sales dramatically, but the most important thing is that you don't have to do anything. If the ranking of your product increases then it will appear higher and have a lot of visibility, which will lead to a lot of new sales without needing you to change anything about the product.

# CHAPTER 15

# Brand Promotion

Your item needs to have an exceptional identity, which the customers can relate to. This, combined with quality services, will influence loyalty amongst your clients, and they'll keep coming back to buy from you. You ought to identify your product from others in the market by making little changes to it and customizing it.

How you select to brand your product depends on the kind of product you are offering. For some products, it may be as simple as attaching a label on the product, while for others, you might have to put more effort, like getting a logo stamped on the product during the making of the product itself.

You can include a hand-made card in your product bundle. This assists in psychological bonding with the customer because of individual differences.

When it comes to upgrading your business, you can do so many things such as; start a blog or a website for the product and switch the traffic to the Amazon site. You can as well insert an e-store on your website, so you can straight offer from there. You can likewise make people register for your newsletter. If it's intriguing, people will leave you their email addresses, which you can use for advertising purposes.

Below are few points to get you in the exact state of mind for promotion:

Branding is not an unneeded cost. It's a financial investment that assists you to sell more.

When starting, prevent spending large quantities on promotion.

When choosing on a trademark name and a logo design, consider what your consumers like, not what you want. Do a substantial research study to come up with the right name and logo design.

Ensure your logo looks polished and professionally developed. Unskilled logos send incorrect signals.

If all your items deal with the same audience, keep them under the same brand. If they belong to various specific niches, it's better to brand name them differently.

It's okay not to name all of your products in the beginning. Do it with one product and as soon as you're making constant earnings, brand other items too.

As soon as there's a name for your brand in the market, you should start promoting it, offered you have sufficient revenues. Start marketing your product by utilizing PPC (Pay Per Click), SEO (Search Engine Optimization), and other techniques. Today, there is plenty of ways to promote.

You also need to consider services like "Amazon Product Ads." Amazon will develop customized advertisements for you and target the right consumers. You'll be charged on a PPC basis, much like other services. Google Adwords is also a fantastic PPC service.

"Amazon Webstore Service" is a quick way to produce a professional-looking website for your products. It's connected to your Seller Central account, so you can get a full combination with all the services and tools you utilize on Amazon.

## Ending Up Being a Top Seller

There are lot of sellers in the marketplace for almost any item. Getting clients' attention is tough because of the rate of competition. So how do you get an edge?

For this, you have to comprehend Amazon's "buy box" algorithm. This algorithm chooses which seller gets the first right to offer if a consumer straight clicks on "Add to cart" after searching for an item. The seller who triumphs the buy box is called the top seller. The consumers can choose to try to find other sellers; however, in many cases, they don't. They buy from the default seller.

Some sellers may be near the client, and some might be selling more customized items. The "buy box" seller automatically sells the most.

Producing a brand identity gives you a golden chance to win the "buy box." You need to invest more in marketing, but it's advantageous in the long run. Winning the buy box gives you sales a substantial increase, so always go for customized branding when you can. Here are some pointers to become a leading seller on Amazon.

## Quality products

It's the best method to get a good ranking for your item. Satisfy your customers with fantastic products, and they'll offer you good reviews.

## Prompt shipping

As soon as you receive an order, deliver the product at the earliest. Customers hate late shipments, so if you want them to return, don't give them a sour experience. Always ship on time.

## Fair rates

Do not increase your items too expensive. You might make significant earnings in the beginning; however, your sales volume will suffer. To end up being a top seller, cut your profit margins a bit because low prices bring in clients.

## Customer satisfaction

Getting excellent consumer reviews requires an effort to keep consumers delighted. As a seller, you must keep a good product rating since even a single unfavourable review will affect your sales significantly in the beginning. Consistently handle your clients calmly and enjoyably, and utilize an e-mail auto-responder to shoot fast first responses to customer emails.

## Top-quality pictures

Always use top-quality pictures for your items and make sure you record it from a variety of angles. The customers require to get a good feel for it before they purchase it. Work with a professional photographer yourself and understand them clicked if you can't get expertly clicked images for your product.

## Product descriptions

As we have currently gone over, writing compelling item descriptions is crucial. It provides your potential clients a push and transforms them into real customers. Compose in-depth stories for your items and make them customer-oriented.

## Handling problems

The consumers at Amazon don't hesitate to file a complaint if they are unhappy with their experience and Amazon is the king of customer service.

So ensure you handle all your consumer grievances in a fast and affordable way. Amazon regularly takes a look at the situation with no bias, so you need to remain in the clear. Consistently please your consumers, and your ratings will stay high.

Everything you do is simply a means to an end here, the purpose being favorable customer reviews. You might hear about people utilizing gray-market strategies like paid reviews. If captured, your Amazon account may be terminated and the company you developed with so much hard work will collapse in seconds.

Often, it will be challenging to end up being a top seller, which's okay. It just implies that your specific niche is too competitive and you need to switch to a less competitive one to become a leading seller.

## The Importance of Building an Email List

One of the most unusual ways to promote your products is through your website and, supplying it is a great one; you will be able to direct more traffic than you ever dreamed possible, not just to your site but on to your Amazon product page. If you have more than a single product for sale, this is even more important.

The Amazon FBA specific niche has got everything you desire-- an audience that is compulsive about purchasing items, social network websites at your disposal, blogs, and platforms that are ideal for

reaching your target audience. You get to drive traffic to your website and your page by talking about blog posts and on forums. You can set up a Facebook page or Twitter account and do the same thing, or talk about other pages that are influential and related.

You can go to other blogs for Amazon FBA and get some concepts for material on your blog, then compose it much more significant, much better, and much bolder to make sure you stand apart. Offered you do this best, your audience will grow and so will your profits. By getting together with others in this niche and networking, you can share their material, link to their blog and see your site grow-- and most will return the favour.

**Among the essential things that you must do before you start with your Amazon FBA product is to construct an email list. These are individuals that you can lawfully target with your product and you can develop a secure connection with them and watch them get the word out for you. This is among the most prominent parts to promoting your organization and one of the most crucial:**

**How to Get Started**

**To start with, you need:**

An excellent website: You can start with a free one or you can spend for one. Make confident that it looks expert and that your material is pertinent and kept up to date-- post frequently.

The very best kind of site, to begin with, is a blog site and you can do with a free WordPress account

An excellent, dependable web hosting:

The free ones use a host however you are better off browsing for one that is reliable a great and brandable domain.

A reasonable premium WordPress or StudioPress theme.

Excellent images and photos-- Either take your own or use those that are royalty-free. If you wish to utilize those that are not royalty-free, you will need to contact the owner for authorization or purchase the image.

An excellent auto-responder: to help you in developing up your e-mail list and to keep in contact with your consumers

A great email capture tool to assist you in growing your email list very rapidly

Your highest top priority is to build up a substantial healthy email list if you are a lethal major about developing up your organization. This is the one property that you have total control over and among the most excellent methods to begin is by having the right presence on social media. You should also be intending for a high ranking on the search engines, especially Google.

Nevertheless, both of these need you to keep up to date with the modifications in algorithms that the likes of Google and Facebook are continuously generating. Your email list is various-- that I yours and no one can take it away from you and no one can alter it.

You must utilize your site and your social network pages to draw in attention to tempt individuals to visit your website and to follow you. You require to motivate them to complete your opt-in form and register to your e-mail list. Once they have done this, you can call them by email, because they have permitted you to do so – be careful not to flood their inboxes with excessive mails; even though they have signed up, this can still be thought about as spam and it can make you a very black mark against your name.

## Beginning-- The Basics of Building an Email List

To obtain on the roadway to constructing up a decent e-mail list, one that can be used to promote your Amazon FBA products, there are numerous things you require to do. The following list covers the outright, standard tasks you need to do to stand any chance of success:

### - Find a Good Email Marketing Service

And register to it. I will assume that you have not yet got an e-mail service company because we are starting right at the very beginning. These will provide you all of the tools that you require, the design templates to utilize, and the services that are essential to getting you the right customers to check out your sales and marketing project and to handle all of the everyday tasks that your list needs.

There are a lot of e-mail service providers to select from, and each will have variable pricing models. You must do your research study carefully here and picks the right service for the list size you desire to construct and the growth that you plan to take place.

Some providers charge a low cost monthly, based on the size of your list, and others will charge you for the number of e-mails that are sent. When you are beginning out is one called MailChimp, one of the most exceptional free services to use.

### - Come Up with the Right Temptation

Before anyone offers you their e-mail address, they are going to want something for it. You have to create the ideal offer, something that will be tempting into signing up for your e-mail list. This might be a free present, an eBook, access to a hot webinar, discount rates, anything that is tempting enough to reel them in. You could reword several pieces of your material, turning them into how-to guides or resources lists. Whatever you do, whatever use you make, it needs to be engaging and it needs to be something that is seen as having a genuine worth.

## - Create Your Opt-In Form

No matter which email company you choose, it will supply you with all the tools you require to develop your opt-in type to go on your site. In basic, you ought to keep it to basics, request for the minimum quantity of information, such as first name and email address just. Your possibility is even more likely to sign up if you are not requesting reams of data. Clearly, you need their email address and merely seeking their given name indicates that you can send out customized e-mails and provides to them. Your possibilities of conversion will drop rapidly and you will not acquire any information that could be thought about vital if you ask for more information than this.

## - Insert the Opt-In Form on Your Website

**This is relatively easy to do and typically involves absolutely nothing more than copying a piece of code, provided by your service provider, and after that pasting it to your website. The positioning of the type is crucial-- you want it where it can be seen but not so that it subdues the rest of your material. The majority of people tend to put it in the right-hand man sidebar, a location that has been proven to have the most excellent**

**conversion rate. Nevertheless, you can place it anywhere you like and the seven best and most magnificent transforming put on your site are:**

Into a special function box

At the really top of the sidebar

At the end of each piece of content or article

In the footer of your website

Put on your About Us or Contact Us Page

Across the upper part of the page in a little bar. WordPress comprises plugins that can assist you with this in a box that pops up

Each of these will carry out differently, depending on your audience, the specific niche you are in and your site. Check out great deals of various

Places to see what works most beautiful and what pulls in the most sign-ups.

Ensure that you offer new subscribers to your list with easy access to the deal you are using to lure them into signing up. If it is an eBook, a webinar, or another piece of content, provide them a download link on the page that they will be sent to when they have validated their email address to you. If it is a discount rate of purchase, make sure you provide them with the appropriate code or details that they need to declare the discount rate.

## --The Next Step-- Getting People to Subscribe

Now that you have gotten that, prepare to collect your email addresses, the tough part begins. Many people will need to put in a bit of severe graft here and start looking outside of their existing audience to build up your list.

### - Use Lists from Other People

Think about offering something in return for having somebody else plug your service on his or her site. You will not be able to attach them in your newsletter but you can use other opportunities for promo-- your website if you already get god levels of traffic, your social media accounts, etc.

### - Add Your Opt-In Form to Another Form

There is a high chance that your site currently contains types on it, such as registrations, contact, kinds for requesting quotes, entries to contests, etc. If your site has any sort on it already, you can add an opt-in box into it. Since your visitors are currently clearly interested in what you are using, this is a fantastic and easy way to develop your email list.

### - Have a Contest or a Giveaway

If you do this right, contests and gifts can be an excellent way of generating new leads among those that are highly targeted. If you currently have the right audience on your social media accounts but you can bring in entrants in other methods as well, this will work better.

The very best method is to offer a giveaway of something vital to your target audience. You can provide away or provide the opportunity to win items that are associated with your specific niche; however, take care that you are not drawing in individuals who are only interested in the reward, not the rest of what you need to offer.

These are some of the most elegant ways to draw in people to your website and fill in your opt-in form. If something does not work, find another way, don't be disappointed. There are a lot of things to try, do not attempt them all at as soon as. Low and steady does win the race here; trying to do too much will ensure that you burn and crash.

# CONCLUSION

Amazon is one of the leading companies of online stores in the world, and it is easy to see why: They have products that many customers did not know they needed, and it is usually at an unbeatable price. Since its beginning, Amazon has been completely devoted to its loyal customer base, and it has only expanded the savings for loyal customers by offering incentives such as Amazon Prime.

With all the sales that Amazon generates every month, it only makes sense to take a part of that pie. After all, if anyone can learn this, you can. Third-party sellers make up more than half of the selling companies on Amazon, and they command a whopping three times the number of products. There is always room for more products in Amazon's massive warehouse collection, and you should be one of the many sellers who can make a living from selling products.

So, do you have what it takes? If you completed this book, then it is obvious that you do. The most difficult part of Amazon FBA is becoming a motivated seller that can take the frustration that may come from sales (or lack thereof) and turn it around. Even if you believe that this does not describe you, we promise that you can get there. All it takes is a little elbow grease and a lot of heart.

Why would you want to sign up with Amazon FBA when there are other options out there and you are just starting out? Amazon has created a third-party selling model that has inspired thousands of other businesses, and they have only refined their practices, so you know that you are getting the most out of the business.

Developing a mindset that will propel you through the most difficult times in your seller journey is absolutely vital. Luckily, we proved that you can find motivation in anything, even setbacks. Find only the best information on the internet and books and sift through the stuff that either makes you waste your time or ends up completely wrong. Believe us, we have seen both sides of that equation. As soon as you find your center with the right information, you can start to build your vision through careful planning and goals. Create your vision from your passions, and it will become easier to be motivated in the future. Once you have set up your goals, keep at them and renew them every time they expire. If you do not meet the goal you had hoped, try again. There is no expiration date for success.

Amazon is responsible for the majority of the work in your professional relationship, which frees up your time to do the things necessary to grow your business. As soon as you send your products to Amazon, they file your products away in a warehouse awaiting a customer. As soon as there is a bite, they send your product to the customer, all of which is done with the Prime shipping plan. Customers get two-day shipping and you get the peace of mind knowing that you did not have to do anything else. Amazon is in charge of customer service and your payment, and all you have to do is keep that inventory stocked for more customers.

Just as with any other company, there are advantages and disadvantages to working with Amazon FBA. If you like the idea of selling but do not want to handle all the customer interaction that goes with it, Amazon FBA is an excellent choice for you. They also offer discounted shipping rates for their professional account holders, which means you can ship packages to Amazon much cheaper than it would cost for you to send them out yourself. Amazon also manages all returns and customer complaints unless there is something wrong with the product. Amazon has potentially unlimited storage space (if you have the money to keep all of it stocked) and promises quick delivery to and from the Amazon warehouse. Amazon also includes a multi-channel fulfillment option that allows you to sell products from your own site.

CPSIA information can be obtained
at www.ICGtesting.com
Printed in the USA
LVHW021707011220
672997LV00006B/732